From the Jaws of Death

Memoirs

Of

James "Doc" McHenry

Prisoner-of-War

and a

Founder of Minneapolis, Kansas

Edited by

Ronald D. Parks

Marvin B. Ballou

From the Jaws of Death

Copyright 2019 by Ronald D. Parks and Marvin B. Ballou

All rights reserved. No part of this book may be reproduced or transmitted in any form or by any means without written permission of the authors.

ISBN # 9781095654798

Published by

Kindle Direct Publishing

All historical photographs used in this book are believed to be in the public domain. No copyright infringements are intended.

Dedications

Ron: To my father, Carroll Parks, WWII veteran and resident of the Solomon valley who embodied the spirit of James McHenry.

Marvin: To my grandmother, Essie Bourne Ballou, who tried to impart her lifelong love of history.

Acknowledgements

We would like to recognize the following people for their generous contributions of time, expertise, and moral support in helping us to compile and edit this book: Ron Brubaker, director of the Minneapolis Public Library; Jettie Condray, former director of the Ottawa County Historical Museum; Samantha Davis, current director of the Ottawa County Historical Museum; LuAnn and Rex Getz, Manhattan; Marilyn Heck, Ottawa County register of deeds, and her deputy, Ardel Helget; Leo Oliva, Kansas historian; Judy Parks, Ron's wife; and Marie Ballou, Marvin's wife.

We would also like to acknowledge Tom Markley, who spent countless hours scanning and organizing thousands of old photographs at the Ottawa County Historical Museum.

Contents

1.	Kind-Hearted Doctor of the Solomon Valley	1
2.	Introduction to James McHenry's Memoirs	19
3.	Army Incidents	22
4.	Escape from Prison	
	Chapter I	36
	Chapter II	43
	Chapter III	50
	Chapter IV	58
	Chapter V	67
	Chapter VI	80
	Chapter VII	88
	Chapter VIII	103
	Chapter IX	114
	Chapter X	123
	Chapter XI	133
	Chapter XII	146
5.	Appendices	162 & 164

Maps

Points of Interest Related to Dr. McHenry in the Solomon Valley   18

Civil War Battles Western Theater   34

Civil War Battles Eastern Theater   35

James McHenry's Trip Home from Prison   159

Civil War Battles of the 22nd Illinois Infantry   163

Prisoner of War Camps Where James McHenry Was Held   165

Preface

With the assistance of several generous people who share our passion for the history of the lower Solomon River valley, the editors of *From the Jaws of Death* have employed historical documents such as newspapers, courthouse records, ledger books, and local histories to retrieve and reconstruct the story of a fascinating and influential man who has been almost forgotten by the passage of time—James "Doc" McHenry.

The centerpiece of this book is McHenry's memoir about his eighteen months incarcerated in Confederate prisoner-of-war camps, which he entitled "Escape from Prison." Arranged in twelve chapters, the series of articles was published in two Minneapolis newspapers from March through November of 1883. This compelling narrative focuses primarily on McHenry's short-lived experiences as a fugitive escapee and the five months he spent in the notorious Salisbury, North Carolina prison. Three years later, McHenry augmented his memoirs in "Army Incidents," an article recounting his experiences at the Battle of Corinth, fought in May of 1862.

From the Jaws of Death begins with a sketch of McHenry's post-Civil War life in Minneapolis, Kansas where in 1867 he established a successful medical practice which lasted until his death in 1890. We then move to his account of the Battle of Corinth and end with his longer narrative pieces about his imprisonment.

McHenry was one of over 600 Union Army veterans who settled in Ottawa County in north-central Kansas. These men and their families transplanted their values, habits, and world views to their new home on the central plains. Consequently, the arc of history connecting the Civil War to the Solomon River valley both past and present is still well marked: townships and streets named Stanton, Sherman, Grant, Sheridan, Logan, and Lincoln; tombstones, grave markers and obelisks in cemeteries bearing memorial inscriptions; and observances of Thanksgiving Day, Memorial Day, and Presidents' Day are all linked to the Civil War era. These ex-soldier settlers left behind not only physical reminders of their presence here, but also established an enduring cultural legacy including Republican Party political dominance, fierce allegiance to the national government, embrace of universal education, a resolute Protestant work ethic, and a determination that their generation's enormous sacrifices would not be forgotten.

Approximately 600,000 soldiers died in the Civil War, the bloodiest war in American history. Death was a constant presence in the United States during the last half of the 19th Century. Contagious diseases, ineffective medical practices, and high rates of infant and maternal mortality contributed to an average life expectancy of 42 years. Both death and prospective death loom large in James McHenry's memoirs of the Civil War. Death was a stark and ever-present fact of his medical practice in the Solomon valley. And death took his wife at age 32 and three of their four offspring in early childhood. We know that McHenry knows of what he speaks when in his memoir he twice employs the poet Tennyson's famous phrase, "The Jaws of Death."

Kind-Hearted Doctor of the Solomon Valley

Soon after the surrender of the Confederate States in April 1865, Private James McHenry suddenly appeared at his home in Sparta, Illinois, where members of his family—having been informed six months earlier of his death in a Confederate prison camp—received him in joyous disbelief. After a period of convalescence, he took courses at the St. Louis Medical College, then headed west to the Kansas frontier, arriving in Salina on July 4, 1867. A few days later, the 28-year-old James "Doc" McHenry journeyed up the Solomon River valley to Minneapolis, then a raw frontier settlement consisting of a saw mill, flour mill, one store, a blacksmith shop, and about a half dozen houses. Here he established a home and medical practice in Minneapolis that would last for the remainder of his life.[1]

Demonstrating the self-reliance and thriftiness required of early settlers, most of whom were impoverished, he shaved the split-out sections of oak into shingles to cover the roof of his newly built office at the corner of Mill and First streets. He quickly became a leader of the tiny community. At the time, all the prominent citizens were given nicknames by their cronies who were always inventing ways to have fun. Because his peers considered him the chief, McHenry became "Sitting Bull," a nickname that clung to him for a long time.[2]

The Civil War veteran had once again landed in a zone of conflict, as in the late 1860s bands of Cheyenne, Arapaho, and Sioux warriors contested the advancement of the railroad up the Smoky

Hill valley in west-central Kansas and the expansion of white settlements up the Solomon valley. At the time, this area was still inhabited by large, but diminishing herds of bison, and the tribes recognized the coming of the white Americans meant the end of their ancient and vitally important bison hunts.

In mid-August of 1868, Indians suddenly attacked settlers at various points between the tiny settlement of Sumnerville (about midway between Delphos and Minneapolis) and Willow Springs (present-day Beloit). Responding to calls for medical assistance, McHenry headed up the Solomon valley escorted by a small party of armed men. Upon reaching the vicinity of Indian Lookout--about two-thirds of the way from Minneapolis to Delphos--they watched as in the distance a small band of Indians approached a wagon train loaded with settlers. As the Indians drew near the train, McHenry saw "the women and children running and screaming over the prairies." Some of his party, raising "an ear-splitting yell," dashed after the Indians, who retreated to the hills west of Delphos.[3]

After reaching Fisher Creek, McHenry learned that two physicians had already proceeded him up the valley and that he was needed at Bond's Corral, a small fort built of prairie sod on the site of present-day Glasco. Here he attended to traumatized settlers who told him "many stories of their hair-breadth escapes from death and outrage." A council was held, and the group decided to evacuate the place after midnight and head down the valley to Minneapolis.[4]

When they reached the vicinity of Indian Lookout the next morning, McHenry and two others searched the prairie where they had last seen the women and children fleeing in terror. After some time, a child jumped up from the grass and ran away screaming, stopping only after they had repeatedly called out that they were not Indians. Then, "at once it appeared as if the ground opened, and women and children sprang up all around us. Great were their expressions of joy." After slaking their intense thirst at a well near Sumnerville, the refugees were transported to Minneapolis, where "there was many a glad reunion of parents and children, husbands and wives, who thought each other murdered by Indians."[5]

When the Indians resumed their raids in October 1868, once again Doc McHenry tended to the wounded, this time extracting a bullet from the body of James S. Morgan, whose wife, Anna, had been captured during the raid. In response to the Indian raids of June 1869 near Indian Lookout, Doc McHenry dispatched a message to the governor appealing for arms, ammunition, and men.[6]

McHenry's participation in the "Indian Raids" of 1868 and 1869 is but one facet of his short but remarkable life in the Solomon valley. He is also distinguished by his civic involvement, patriotism, courage, physical suffering, political independence, spiritual non-conformity, and unrelenting cheerfulness and generosity in the face of a series of personal tragedies.

In early June of 1870, Doc McHenry purchased from the Kansas Pacific Railroad forty acres of rolling prairie on the north bank of the Solomon River near its confluence with Pipe Creek. A few days later the plat of the "Original Town Minneapolis," laid out and hand drawn by James McHenry, was recorded. Soon after, McHenry deeded off lots to Elijah Smith, A. C. Stull, Israel Markley, Jacob Campbell and others. Later that same year, when the Minneapolis Printing Association was organized to raise money to start a weekly county newspaper, the first name listed on the Committee for Subscription of Stocks was Dr. J. McHenry.[7]

As was the practice of many pioneer doctors, McHenry established his own drug store. It was located at the corner of First and Mill streets, the epicenter of Minneapolis during those early village years. In the late 1870s, Doc placed an ad in the *Minneapolis Independent* calling attention to the fact that he was the "proprietor of the oldest established drug store in the Solomon Valley." In March 1879, he moved into his new stone drug store on the north side of Second Street, which by then had become the main commercial thoroughfare of Minneapolis. The *Minneapolis Independent* sung the praises of its "elegant style. The wood work is artistically grained in red oak and walnut . . . . The entire store has a pleasing, light and recherché appearance, and demonstrates the doctor's good taste and progressive ideas." Among the many items offered at Doc McHenry's drug store was the "mild, fragrant and delicious" Marble Head cigar. In the basement patrons could take baths at all hours and get a haircut. The centerpiece of the store, however, was the beautiful, eight-foot-long soda fountain made of white marble that Doc had bought for $450.00. "Ice soda water always on draught at Dr. McHenry's" proclaimed an ad. During his lifetime, McHenry accumulated many friends but little wealth. Described by a medical colleague as "kind-hearted to a fault," Doc frequently would write a prescription for an impoverished person, then give his patient the money to pay for the medicine at the drug store.[8]

By the early 1880s, he had sold his drug store and was practicing medicine from an office on Second Street. At about this time, there were six licensed physicians in the town of about one thousand residents. In 1880, Doc left Minneapolis for several months to attend courses at the Kansas City Medical College. By April 1881, he returned to Minneapolis and resumed his medical practice.[9]

Minneapolis Second Street late 1800s

McHenry admonished the town's residents not to throw "slops, dish waters and other kitchen refuse in the ground" as such would "give birth immediately to millions of similar miasms until the air is fully impregnated for miles around." The "miasma theory," a standard medical belief of Doc's era long since discredited, attributed many diseases such as cholera to miasma, a noxious form of "bad air" emanating from rotting organic matter.[10]

Pioneer doctors were mostly helpless before the germ-borne afflictions of the pre-bacteriological age. Reflecting on his early medical career, Kansas pioneer doctor Arthur Hertzler ruefully observed that "the medicines I dispensed were merely symbols of good intentions." Among these medicines were large supplies of quinine, opium, nux vomica, castor oil, and whisky. One of the favorite medicines of that era was calomel, a mercury compound believed by many physicians to be a cure-all. In fact, excessive use of this drug had injurious effects, especially on children and adolescents, which include deterioration of teeth, jaw bones, palate and tongue.[11]

Many of the beliefs on which McHenry and his colleagues had based their medical practices started to crumble in the 1880s, the decade of the "reign of the microbes." Between 1880 and 1900, researchers investigating bacteriology discovered the germs that caused diphtheria and typhoid fever, as well as tuberculosis, cholera, and many other diseases. Medicine became more of a science. In the early years of Kansas settlement, the great killers of young children were digestive and bowel ailments caused mostly by impure milk and infected water. This meant that the most effective antidote for the high infant death-rate was prevention through pure water and sterile milk. Surgeons gradually realized that it was clothes, instruments, sheets, and their own hands rather than the air in the operating room which brought the disease-bearing germs to the patient. Wearing filthy surgical aprons and espousing the benefits of pus receded into the past. Soap and rigid cleanliness became the standard modes of operation.[12]

Because his medical practice encompassed all of Ottawa County, Glasco, Beloit, and points further up the Solomon valley, Doc McHenry journeyed long distances to administer to his patients. His primary means of conveyance was horse and buggy. Day and night, in all kinds of weather and road conditions, Doc McHenry was, according to the *Solomon Valley Pioneer*, "always ready to go at a moments warning to the head of the Solomon, or anywhere else, where suffering humanity require." Another Kansas horse and buggy doctor, Arthur Hertzler, described what it was like to "hitch up, plug along the roads, make a call, plug back again at the same old weary pace. Get stuck in the mud, get out somehow, meet a snowdrift, shovel out or cut the fence and drive around the obstruction." Doc's fees were determined, in part, by the distance he traveled to reach his patients. Minneapolis residents were charged $1.50 for in-home visits. On the other hand, McHenry charged the Spitzer family, who resided on the Saline River about twelve miles from Minneapolis, ten dollars for each of four visits in late November 1874. Most payments, if made at all, were in cash, but some paid their medical bills by delivering firewood or bushels of corn.[13]

Oftentimes, pioneer doctors could do little for their in-home patients besides offering palliatives such as cold-sponging a delirious patient back to consciousness, a frequently long and tedious practice whose main value was to provide comfort to the family members and friends present in the home. According to one of McHenry's medical colleagues, Doc McHenry's ultra-sympathetic nature regarding his patients, especially children, sometimes limited his ability to perform his professional duties. Minneapolis physician William Campbell recalled that many times Doc called on him "to set broken limbs and perform other surgical operations on his patients, his sympathies being such as to require him to seek assistance, as he could not bear to hear the screams of the suffering."[14]

Aside from his professional commitments, McHenry also contributed to his community by joining several civic and fraternal organizations. He served on the Minneapolis Board of Health and as a U.S. examining surgeon for pensions. He was a trustee of the Minneapolis International Order of the Odd Fellows (IOOF), which at the time was the largest fraternal organization in the United States. He also was a member of the Freemasons and the Kansas State Historical Society.[15]

During the early 1880s, Doc befriended a young African-American who resided in Minneapolis named George Washington Carver. McHenry hired George to do a variety of tasks and loaned the studious young man books from his library. Carver went on to achieve international fame as an acclaimed agricultural scientist and educator.[16]

In February of 1879, Minneapolis was put on high alert when about sixty Ponca and Omaha Indians were reported "swarming in town," then established a camp on Lindsey Creek. Once again, McHenry notified the governor of Kansas, this time by means of the recently installed telegraph. The next morning the Indians decamped without incident.[17]

Though a pillar of his community, the well-liked McHenry did not shy away from controversy, and his political positions usually ran counter to the mainstream. A year after Kansas voters in 1880 had approved an amendment to the state constitution banning the production, sale, and purchase of alcoholic beverages--an act supported by the majority of Ottawa County voters--McHenry wrote a lengthy column in a Minneapolis newspaper stating his strong objections to the Prohibition Law. "I do not believe," McHenry declared, "that the judicious use of alcoholic stimulants is an unmitigated evil, nor do I believe that total abstinence or prohibition to be the sum of all virtue." Like any dissident, Doc would pay a price. On November 3, 1882, the *Minneapolis Sentinel* insinuated that Dr. McHenry attended "a certain den on Second Street, where secret meetings are held and sealed with whisky and beer."[18]

When he first arrived in Ottawa County in 1867, Doc, like most Union Army veterans, was a Republican. However, McHenry detested Ulysses Grant, the commanding general of the Union armies in the late years of the Civil War, and he abandoned the party when Grant, who was a Republican, occupied the White House from 1869 through 1877. By the late 1870s, McHenry had become a local leader of the Greenbackers, a party of left-wing populists that enjoyed some electoral success both locally and nationally from 1878 through 1882. He continued to align with third-party politics, joining the Anti-Monopolist Party in the mid-1880s and the Union Labor Party in the late 1880s. The platform of the latter party advocated a series of progressive policies including the radical notion of granting women the right to vote in all elections. Seeking to curb the power of corporations and enhance the financial status of the poorer classes, the Union Labor party advocated ending government aid to railroads, redemption of mortgaged property, abolition of interest on public debt, and the adoption of six percent maximum interest rates.[19]

Doc also joined the Knights of Labor, a radical labor union that wielded considerable political power on a national scale in the early and mid-1880s. He was, according to the *Commercial*, "always on the side of the poor and distressed." He felt that the national political leadership had betrayed the interests of the people and democracy. "For the support of a wealthy corporate power or monopoly," McHenry wrote, "they [politicians] have already granted powerful franchises that are incompatible in their nature, with free institutions."[20]

He held the office of surgeon in the local chapter of the Grand Army of the Republic (GAR), the large and powerful organization of Union Army veterans. Although nominally non-partisan, the GAR was, in practice, almost always politically aligned with the Republican Party. A political maverick with impeccable veteran credentials, James McHenry challenged this arrangement, as the Republican *Minneapolis Sentinel* made clear in November of 1882: "Dr. McHenry always seems very much worried for fear the reunions [GAR] are gotten up for political purposes. He seems to be afraid that people will put it into their heads that Union soldiers and the Republican Party have some slight affiliations." Many facets of the visionary politics of James McHenry and his "radical" allies in the Solomon valley were to come to fruition in the reforms adopted by the Populist Party (1890-1896); Theodore Roosevelt Republicans (1901-1913); New Deal Democrats (1933-1941); and Lyndon Johnson's Great Society (1964-1969). In essence, all of these reformers advocated using government as an instrument to ensure that all Americans were endowed with political rights and economic opportunities. In each of these interludes, progressive candidates in local, state, and federal elections received substantial support from north-central Kansas voters.[21]

McHenry's independent nature also manifested in his spiritual life. "I have always been more or less troubled by the disease, agnosticism," he wrote. "In fact, I am sort of a doubting Thomas." Doc was amused that although he was "not much of anything, especially in a religious, or Christian sense," he found it strange that throughout his life some of his best and truest friends were

Methodist clergymen. "He was a free thinker and somewhat cynical," wrote the *Solomon Valley Democrat*. "But he was whole-souled and liberal hearted." Occasionally, McHenry would journey to Lawrence to seek out the companionship of fellow Freethinkers at the assembly of Liberals at Bismarck Grove. Here, he was reportedly "highly satisfied by the intellectual feast he enjoyed there."[22]

Despite his unorthodoxies, James McHenry remained woven into the fabric of the community because of, in part, his fun-loving nature. The *Solomon Valley Pioneer* referred to him and two of his colleagues as "three as jolly jokers as ever shouldered a pair of pill bags." Another newspaper claimed Doc's footraces against other prominent citizens were "the most enlivening and mirth producing amusement" in town. Weighing at least 250 pounds, McHenry, even when given substantial head-starts, seemed to lose every race. In June of 1879, a one-block-long race on Second Street pitted McHenry against Mayor George McKenzie, who supported a large girth as well. The doctor started well but the mayor overtook him and, according to the tongue-in-cheek *Minneapolis Sentinel*, "was the winner by several 'breadths,' which, by the way, was no small distance." Stakes were ice cream, liberally supplied by the loser to all present.[23]

At the age of 34, James married 17-year-old Amelia Victoria Stewart in June of 1873. The couple lived in a house on First Street where Amelia, or "Millie," gave birth to four children. Like many area residents, the Stewarts and the McHenrys were supported by extended families. Amelia's widowed mother, Jane, lived near her son, John H. Stewart, and a daughter, Sarah, and their families in Garfield Township northwest of Minneapolis, and Doc McHenry's brother and sister both moved from Illinois to Minneapolis in the 1880s.[24]

James and Amelia McHenry were stalked by tragedy. Three of their children died in early childhood. Perhaps to escape painful memories, Doc sold his house on First Street in 1884 and built a new residence on the northwest corner of Laurel and Rothsay. (This house still stands at that location though modified over time.) One evening in February of 1888, Amelia's mother, while walking home from a visit to a neighbor, apparently became disoriented and died in the middle of a pasture. Three months later Amelia, after a sudden onset of illness, died the next day, leaving her 10-year-old daughter, Carlotta, and husband James "sorely afflicted." A few days after Amelia's death, James suffered a severe stroke from which he never fully recovered.[25]

McHenry house in Minneapolis

After a brief visit to his boyhood home in Illinois, Doc McHenry returned to Minneapolis somewhat improved in health. During the last year of his life he remained politically active, attending a "Tariff Reformers" meeting in October of 1889, unsuccessfully running for the office of county coroner on the Union Labor ticket in November, and writing a column in the *Bennington Star* in support of a local Union Labor candidate. He also spent many of his final days visiting old friends. He was reported to be in Delphos, Ada, and Beloit reminiscing about the early days in the Solomon valley, doing a little politicking, and, one suspects, saying his last good-byes.[26]

During the rigors of his wartime imprisonment, Doc had contracted diseases of the heart and lungs from which he suffered for the remainder of his life. In mid-January of 1890, he was attacked by "la grippe," a common term at that time for influenza. This led to pneumonia and he died on January 28 at the age of 51. A large crowd attended the funeral at the McHenry home on Laurel and Rothsay, and a long line of buggies, wagons, and carriages formed the procession east to Highland Cemetery where his remains were interred beside Amelia's grave. The simple engraving on his small, unpretentious grave marker--the standard tombstone for thousands of veterans in cemeteries throughout the nation--is emblematic of the man: "Jas. McHenry, Co. H, 22 Ill. Inf."[27]

Amelia's grave marker

The death of James McHenry evoked an outpouring of heartfelt elegies by the three newspapers published each week in Minneapolis, population 1,700. "He had lots of very warm friends and was liked by everybody," said the *Solomon Valley Democrat*. Dr. McHenry had "a heart as tender towards the suffering as most women," observed the *Minneapolis Commercial*. "Dr. McHenry was the most generous and liberal hearted man we ever knew," the *Messenger* obituary declared. "And all through those years he gave of his strength and money. He was prominent in all matters pertaining to the advancement of the town and county. Every man, woman and child knew Dr. McHenry and to know him was to honor and respect him. Peace to his soul.[28]

ENDNOTES

1. *Minneapolis Commercial*, 2-5-1890; *Minneapolis Messenger*, 11-22-1883.
2. *Commercial*, 2-5-1890; *Messenger*, 7-25-1895.
3. James McHenry, "Historical," *Messenger*, 1-1-1885.
4. *Ibid*.
5. *Ibid*.
6. *Messenger*, 7-18-1889; 2-6-1890; *Leavenworth Times*, 6-15-1869.
7. Records in the office of the Ottawa County Register of Deeds, Courthouse, Minneapolis, Kansas; E-mail from Marilyn Heck, Ottawa County Register of Deeds, to Ron Parks (9-10-2018); *History of Ottawa County, Kansas, 1864-1984*, 163; *Abilene Weekly Chronicle*, 9-1-1870.
8. *Independent*, 9-21-1878; 3-29, 4-5, 4-26, 5-3, 5-10, 5-17-1879; *Commercial* 2-5-1890.
9. *Index*, 12-29-1880; 4-20-1881; *Messenger*, 6-11-1885; 7-4-1907; Birds Eye View Maps of Minneapolis (1875 and 1879*)*.

10. *Independent*, 5-31-1879; Thomas Neville Boner, *The Kansas Doctor: A Century of Pioneering* (Lawrence: University Press of Kansas, 1959), 37.
11. Arthur E. Hertzler, M.D., *The Horse and Buggy Doctor* (Lincoln, Nebr.: University of Nebraska Press, 1938), 78; Boner, 21; Jennifer Schmid, "Beautiful Black Poison," https://www.westonaprice.org/health-topics/environmental-toxins/beautiful-black-poison/, accessed October 25, 2018.
12. Boner, 38, 51, 53, 59, 61-62.
13. *Solomon Valley Pioneer*, 12-6-1870; Hertzler, 79; *McHenry and Dunn's Ledger Books* (April 17, 1871, and December 30, 1873), Ottawa County Historical Museum collection.
14. Hertzler, 78; *Commercial*, 2-5-1890.
15. *Messenger*, 2-12, 6-11-1885; 2-6-1890; *Independent*, 6-2-1877; 6-28-1879; *Index*, 6-6-1883; *Solomon Valley Democrat*, 1-31-1890.
16. Jason H. Gart, Ph.D., *He Shall Direct Thy Paths: The Early Life of George W. Carver*, Historic Resource Study, National Park Service (2014), 67; Linda O. McMurry, *George Washington Carver: Scientist and Symbol*, Oxford University Press (1981), 23.
17. *Independent*, 2-1-1879.
18. *Index*, 11-16-1881, *Minneapolis Sentinel*, 11-3-1882.
19. *Junction City Weekly Union*, 9-5-1868; *Independent*, 11-9-1878; *Messenger*, 9-12-1884; 10-13, 10-20, 1887; *Democrat*, 10-14, 10-21, 1887; *Delphos Republican*, 11-2-1889; James C. Malin, *A Concern About Humanity: Notes on Reform, 1872-1912 at the National and Kansas Levels of Thought* (Ann Arbor, Michigan: Edwards Brothers, 1964), 35.
20. *Index*, 6-6-1883; *Commercial*, 2-5-1890; McHenry, "Escape from Prison," *Messenger*, 11-8-1883.

21. *Messenger*, 12-18-1884; *Sentinel*, 11-3-1882.
22. *Messenger*, 8-15, 11-1-1883; *Index*, 6-6-1883; *Democrat*, 1-31-1890; *Independent*, 9-27-1879.
23. *Solomon Valley Pioneer*, 12-6-1870; *Messenger*, 7-25-1895; 7-4-1907; *Independent,* 6-28-1879.
24. *U.S. Census*, 1860, 1870: *Kansas State Census*, 1875, 1885; *Messenger*, 6-14-1888; 2-6-1890; 9-19-1918; *Commercial*, 2-5-1890.
25. *Messenger*, 2-16, 4-17-1884; 5-24, 6-14-1888; 2-6-1890. [Carlotta N. McHenry ("Lottie") was the only child of four born to James and Amelia McHenry to survive childhood. She married Wilbur W. Robinson. Their only child, James H. Robinson, was born in 1896. The couple divorced in 1901. Lottie married William T. Barker in 1910. James McHenry's brother, Hugh M. McHenry resided in Minneapolis from 1888 until his death in 1924. Hugh and James' sister, Eliza J., lived in Minneapolis from 1887 until 1910 when she moved to the state of Washington. James H. Robinson and William Barker both died in 1952. James Robinson never married and produced no offspring. Carlotta Barker lived her last few years near Ada in Ottawa County, Kansas. She died in 1964.]
26. *Messenger*, 7-7-1887; 7-19, 11-1-1888; 6-13, 8-1, 10-10-1889; *Beloit Gazette*, 6-6-1889.
27. *Messenger*, 2-6-1890; *Commercial*, 2-5-1890; *Democrat*, 1-31-1890.
28. *Democrat*, 1-31-1890; *Commercial*, 2-5-1890; *Messenger*, 2-6-1890.

POINTS OF INTEREST RELATED TO DR. McHENRY IN THE SOLOMON VALLEY

Points of Interest of Dr. McHenry

- ① Anna Morgan Captured
- ② Indian Lookout
- ③ Bond's Corral
- ④ Highland Cemetery
- ⑤ Where Jane Stuart Died
- ⑥ Sumnerville

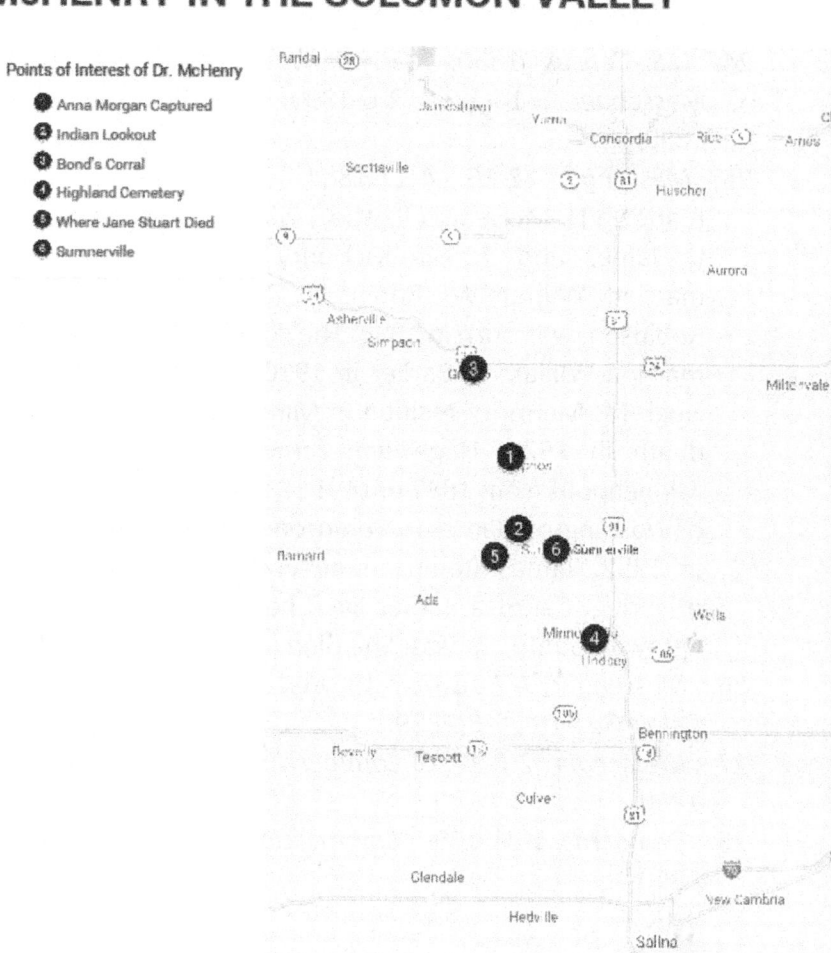

Introduction to James McHenry's Memoirs

Born and raised in Sparta, Illinois, James McHenry left a teaching position to enlist in the Union Army in June of 1861, serving in Company H of the 22nd Illinois Volunteer Infantry. His memoirs of his wartime experiences appeared in articles published in Minneapolis newspapers in the 1880s. A single article published in the *Messenger* on April 8, 1886, "Army Incidents," recounted McHenry's battlefield experiences during the siege of Corinth, Mississippi in early May of 1862. "Escape from Prison" is McHenry's twelve-chapter narrative of his experiences as a prisoner of war in Confederate prison camps. The first installment was published in the *Ottawa County Index* on March 28, 1883, and the final article appeared in the *Minneapolis Messenger* on November 8, 1883.[1] [The editors have sought to retain McHenry's somewhat erratic spelling, punctuation and capitalization in the text excepting instances where his (or the printer's) non- standard usage might perplex the reader.]

These memoirs, however, do not render a complete record of his entire career as a Union Army soldier in the Civil War. In addition to the siege of Corinth, McHenry and his 22nd Illinois regiment saw action in the battles of New Madrid, Island No. 10, Belmont, Shiloh, and lastly--for McHenry--Chickamauga, all of which receive short shrift in "Army Incidents." And although McHenry was held in Confederate prisons over an eighteen-month period, his "Escape from Prison" series focuses primarily on the last six months of his imprisonment [See Appendices A and B].

McHenry was wounded and taken prisoner on September 20, 1863, during the Battle of Chickamauga, the second bloodiest battle of the Civil War. Excepting a brief interval as an escapee, McHenry served time in seven Confederate prisons: Belle Isle and Libby in Richmond, Virginia; Danville, Virginia; Andersonville, Georgia; Florence and Charleston, South Carolina; and Salisbury, North Carolina. While at Andersonville, a slave advised him that to help evade pursuers and their hounds, he should tie pine needles to the soles of his shoes, a ploy he put to good effect when escaping from the Florence prison. He was recaptured and underwent trial for the capital offense of being a spy.[2] While in prison he and his fellow prisoners suffered from, in his words, "Bleak cold winds, and rain without any or adequate shelter, gibbering idiocy, raving insanity, starvation, despair and death, were there all of them shapes hot from hell." At Salisbury, in the face of murderous assaults by a vicious gang of Confederate deserters with whom he was imprisoned, McHenry stood steadfast and survived.

According to historian Charles W. Sanders, Jr., young men in perfect health when they entered the prison stockades would "sicken and die within a space of a few weeks." Sanders listed the immediate causes of death as "overcrowding, exposure, poor sanitation, inadequate medical care, and starvation." Approximately one in seven of all Civil War prisoners died in the prison camps; the death rate for Yankee prisoners was 15.5%; for Rebels it was 12%. The Florence prison camp from which McHenry escaped lost 2,802 of its 12,000 prisoners in four months, a death rate of 23%. About one-third of the prisoners in the Salisbury Camp between October of 1864 and the time of their release in February of 1865 died.[3]

These numbers supply a big picture, but McHenry's narratives provide a detailed, intimate, and unflinching illustration of both the vilest and most benevolent behaviors of men while under the unimaginable stress of confinement in the hellish Confederate prison camps. He is an excellent writer, infusing his narratives with literary allusions, self-deprecating humor, fascinating character sketches of his compatriots, and vivid and detailed accounts of army and prison life. James McHenry emerges from the text as a young man possessing courage, a quick wit, resourcefulness, a love of humanity, and, above all, grit.

1. *U.S. Census*, 1860; Letter from James McHenry to Auditor's Office, Washington D.C., April 7, 1886, Ottawa County History Museum archives.
2. *Commercial*, 2-5-1890; James McHenry, "Escape from Prison," *Messenger*, 10-25-1883; *Ottawa County Index*, 3-28, 7-11-1883.
3. Charles W. Sanders, Jr., *While in the Hands of the Enemy: Military Prisons of the Civil War* (Baton Rouge: Louisiana State University Press, 2005), 1-5, 253-255; Louis A. Brown, *The Salisbury Prison: A Case Study of Confederate Military Prisons, 1861-1865* (Wendell, North Carolina: Avera Press, 1980), 119.

ARMY INCIDENTS

Old soldiers, especially those residing in Ottawa County, are invited to contribute short articles, containing personal reminiscences of the war, for this column. Their full name, regiment and company should be given in every case. One of the editors of this paper served a thousand days for "Uncle Sam," and he will avail himself, from time to time, of this invitation when other comrades have not responded. The column belongs to the soldiers, for the purpose stated.

Messrs. Editors:

I will now attempt to keep my half-promise in trying to tell of the time that the rebs used my back for a target. Our brigade was then commanded by Payne, our division by Palmer and our army by Pope.[1] Under Pope, our army had invested New Madrid, and which with immense stores of forage, etc. had fallen into our hands. The unheard of feat, of bringing four transports over the "sunken lands" of New Madrid, had been accomplished and with them, forces had been thrown across the river to intercept the retreating garrison of Island No. 10. They were captured, and this necessitated the falling into our hands of Columbus, KY--the "Gibraltar of the Mississippi." We then dropped down and began the investment of Fort Pillow, but were immediately recalled, and sent up the Tennessee River to Pittsburg Landing, to where Grant's forces came so nearly meeting with a terrible disaster a few days previously. The successes of our army (called then "right wing of the Army of the Mississippi,") under Pope, were then without parallel in the war. Thousands of prisoners and millions of dollars worth of arms, war munitions and forage had fallen into our hands, yet Pope had not as yet shed scarcely a drop of blood of his army, and we had almost begun to fear that Pope would be called to the Generalship of the army and close up the war by out-maneuvering and out-generaling the Johnnies, and we would not get a chance of testing our staying qualities in a regular "stand up and fight." But Pope's forces were marched to the front on one of the roads to Corinth, until at length we were facing a large, boggy swamp, through which meandered a brook. About three-fourths of a mile west from where our road emerged from this swamp was a field and in it a large cotton gin. About 1 1/2 miles to the southwest of the same place in the road, was a little town called Farmington, about five miles east of Corinth, and between the cotton gin and Farmington, there was quite a grove. On the 2nd day of May, '62, we were facing this swamp. On the following morning, the 3rd, where our road crossed the swamp, we were met by a considerable body of rebels, when a brisk skirmish ensued. The rebels retired, leaving several of their dead. Our regiment moved forward and occupied for awhile the spot where three of the rebels had fallen. Some of us dug a wide grave and buried them side by side.

Maj. Francis Swanwick, afterward our Colonel, a brave and great hearted old gentleman, who had a reckless habit of picking up and dropping his "h"s and who used to say he loved me as if I were his son, "because your grandfather hand hi were chums hin the Black Awk war, you know."[2] He found somewhere a nice board and on it he carved this sentence, "Here rests three misguided rebels, who fell on this spot May 3rd, 1862," and placed it at the head of the grave.

As soon as the rebels were driven from this part of the road, a force of engineers, sappers and miners with details of soldiers were put to work and soon there was built a corduroy road across the swamp, when our division was thrown across, and made a reconnaissance past Farmington and almost up to the fortifications of Corinth, but for some reason were ordered back across the swamp to our old position. On the 9th of May our brigade, with some other troops were again ordered across the swamp, and took positions fronting usually south and west. There were large spaces between the regiments. Our regiment occupied a depressed piece of ground in the edge of the grove, south of the cotton gin, and in front of our company was a little dirty pond. At this time, as we afterward learned, Bragg[3] and VanDorn with their forces, came out and offered us battle. It was understood amongst us that Pope was eager to accept the challenge, but for some unaccountable reason, he was holding us back. As the rebel line of skirmishers and line of battle advanced and opened on us, their artillery began to play also. We had strict orders not to return their fire, but lie prone, and to be ready to repel a charge with bayonet. Our regiment was so isolated, that we could not even see any other troops, but our position being on a depression in the ground, and by lying flat, we avoided a perfect storm of artillery and musketry. Just now a body of cavalry began forming on our left, led by Sheridan,[4] then a Colonel. A small body of cavalry came to our right under Gen. Payne. Just then we were ordered to prepare to charge the enemy.

Just then I spoke to Tommy Anderson, our 1st corporal. Between him and me stood Nathaniel Scott, a hero and patriot of other wars and countries, a scholar and philosopher. I said to Tom, "Isn't this a tight fix to get into?" At Belmont Tommy had received several slight wounds, had his clothes literally riddled with balls, and had caught two or three in the stock of his musket, and when I spoke, he said, "yes Jim, but since Belmont, I cannot believe the ball was ever moulded to kill me." These were his last words. Just then I was suddenly blinded. I thought a shell had exploded in the muddy pond in front of us, and had thrown the heated and muddy water in my face, but when I had cleared my eyes, I found it was the blood and brains of poor Tommy Anderson, and his headless body was lying at my feet. The same ball struck Sergeant James Dyer on the neck, severing his head from his body. It was a cannon ball that had done the terrible work. One comrade, when he saw the tragedy, exclaimed, "Oh! My God!" Scott who was, if possible worse covered over than I, just now had cleared his eyes, and saw the work of the ball, soliloquized thus: "Well, I thought a man with that amount of brains ought to have had more sense than to have been caught in a snap like this." At this moment we were ordered to charge the enemy in front with fixed bayonets, which we did with a whoop and a yell. The small bodies of cavalry on our left and right led by Payne and Sheridan hurled themselves like a pair of thunderbolts on the rebels.

We swept back everything before us until we had passed through the grove and into the field beyond, until we reached a portion of a field battery that had been playing on us and was now abandoned. When, to our surprise, we were ordered to halt, and our colonel--

Hart--a taciturn, but brave and kindhearted man from Alton, IL, received peremptory orders from Gen. Payne to move the regiment to the rear, which was immediately done.

When we went into the charge we had unslung our knapsacks. When we had reached our knapsacks Col. Hart halted the regiment and asked of Gen. Payne permission for his men to get their knapsacks. Gen. Payne's order was prompt and to the point: "Wait for nothing, sir. Get your men out of here and stand d---d little on your order of going."

We were fronting south near our knapsacks, and Col. Hart's next order was prompt,--"Right face--by right flank file right--double quick--march." We were marched north across the field, by the cotton gin over the brow of the hill and into the swamp, about three-fourths of a mile above our corduroy road. Perhaps we had not gone over the length of our regiment when rebel bullets began to whistle around us. This had the effect of stimulating our double-quick into a run--a demonstration of the fact, that if not allowed to fight, we could do the other thing. When the first seven companies had cleared the field, and passed over the rather abrupt bank into the swamp, and out of direct range of the enemy's missiles, it seemed as if there was about three batteries and a whole brigade of infantry playing on the tail end of the regiment. About a week previous to this time I had had quite a little spell of sickness and had not quite recovered my usual health, and perhaps, too, even at that early date in my life I carried a little more adipose tissue than I could fully appreciate under the circumstances, so that when the last man of the regiment but me had passed over the brow of the hill, I was about three rods behind him, and for a few seconds had a full benefit, all to myself, and realized fully the force of the old saying relative to the Devil catching the hindmost.

It is related that a rebel cavalry officer and some of his command were rapidly retreating through a lane by his own home, and the lane was being shelled by a Union battery. One of his slaves, an old gray-headed darky preacher, was standing in his cabin door surrounded by other slaves witnessing the scene and listening to the shrieking of the shells as they hustled past, when the old gray-headed preacher raised his hands and exclaimed; "Glory! Glory! Glory to God. De year ob Jubilee am come; yonder runs massa wid the wraf of God after him." Well, when those shells were screaming and bursting around me that day, it did seem an illustration of the darky's idea of what was after his "massa." About this time I heard, or thought I heard, a shell coming directly toward me and I thought it would strike me in the small of the back, so I sprang to the right. My calculation was wrong for it passed me still a few feet to the right and burst about a rod beyond me. This, poetically speaking, seemed to add wings to my speed, for I was soon over the brow of the hill and into the swamp, and out of direct range of the missiles. But here a new trouble presented itself. The rebels were shelling the woods, and the shells would cut off large limbs from the trees and considerable dodging had to be done to avoid them falling on us, and the ground being boggy we had to jump from one tuft of grass or hillock to another to avoid sinking in the bog. After I had penetrated the swamp some two or three hundred yards, and as I was now most terrible tired and thought I was sufficiently far from the rebels, I thought I would take a rest, so I sat down on the end of an old cypress log. The lower part of the log was considerably rotted, but the upper part was quite sound and light and dry. I had no more than sat down until a shell or shot struck the other end of the log and literally knocked it from under me. Here was new inspiration--for I was thrown about a half a rod, but lit on my feet running. I did not pause again until I reached the brook that ran through the swamp, and as it was narrow I sprang across it but sank above my knees in the bog. At first I could not extricate myself, but luckily within my reach there grew a young sapling by which, after divesting myself of my accoutrements, I succeeded at length in pulling myself out, sans shoes, sans stockings, and in fact sans everything excepting a good coating of mud. Soon afterward I reached the edge of the swamp where I found a heavy picket or skirmish line. Some distance behind this was an entrenched line of battle. I now lay down on a green sward in the shade of some trees and put in about an hour of the hardest, solidest rest that I ever enjoyed. I think I never was so tired. After this I wended my way to camp, where most of the boys had preceded me. Ablutions, etc. were in order for the rest of the day.

There were several other casualties occurring in the regiment that day, other than noted, but they occurred during the time we were in position before the charge and during the charge.

I think there was no serious casualty during the retreat across the field and through the swamp.

About this time I had a great ambition to become an expert in handling the "dignitaries of the chess board," and had a set of chessmen and board in my knapsack. Gens. Payne and Palmer had on one or two occasions borrowed it. Next morning, an orderly from Gen. Payne's headquarters came to me and said: "Gen. Payne presents his compliments to you and requests the loan of your chessmen." I replied: "Present my compliments to Gen. Payne and tell him he is entirely welcome, but as they were in my knapsack yesterday, he probably would find them over in the rebel camp today."

General Eleazer Paine

A few days after we occupied a position far beyond the scene of our skedaddle, and in a deserted rebel camp I picked up two or three pieces of my chessmen.

The cause of our being placed in this position and afterward withdrawn, in the face of the enemy, was that Gen. Halleck,[5] then in command, absolutely forbade the bringing on of an engagement. He appeared unwilling to engage the enemy,--already defeated at Shiloh[6]--unless he was behind trenches. He was too cautious. Pity he and Grant had not been "carded" through each other a little in this respect, then we would have had two better generals.

J. McHenry

Company H 22nd Illinois Volunteers

"Army Incidents" End notes

1   Generals *Eleazar Paine*, [McHenry erroneously spells this name "Payne"] *John Palmer*, and *John Pope* led Union forces in the capture of *New Madrid*, Missouri, and *Island Number 10* on the Mississippi River in the spring of 1862. These victories freed the Mississippi River for Union navigation as far south as Memphis. Subsequently, Paine participated in the successful *Siege of Corinth* described by McHenry in "Army Incidents"; Palmer led his troops effectively during the Battle of Chickamauga where McHenry was captured. His post-war career included positions as governor of Illinois, U.S. senator, and presidential candidate for the National Democratic Party in 1896. John Pope was chosen by President Lincoln to lead the Army of Virginia, but was relieved of his command in September 1862 after his Union forces suffered defeat at the Second Battle of Bull Run.

Major General John Palmer

Major General John Pope

2 *Black Hawk War* was fought in 1832 between allied Indian tribes led by the Sauk chief, Black Hawk, and U.S. troops. Battles fought in Illinois and Michigan resulted in a U.S. victory.

3 *Braxton Bragg* (1817-1876) was a Confederate general who commanded an army in the western theater in the early years of the Civil War. He led the defeat of Union forces at the Battle of Chickamauga. *Earl Van Dorn* (1820-1863) was also a Confederate general in the western theater.

4 General *Philip Sheridan* (1831-1888) effectively led the Cavalry Corps of the Army of the Potomac in defeating Confederate forces in the Shenandoah Valley, and later his cavalry pursued General Robert E. Lee, helping to force his surrender at Appomattox.

General Philip Sheridan

5 General *Henry Wager Halleck* was a senior Union Army commander in the western theater early in the war. He was the

field commander at the Siege of Corinth, a significant victory for the Union Army.

6   The *Battle of Shiloh* was fought April 6-7, 1862 in southwestern Tennessee. After both sides sustained heavy casualties, Union troops under the command of Ulysses Grant forced the Confederate army to retreat, thereby creating the opportunity for the Union to advance into northern Mississippi.

Civil War Battles Western Theater

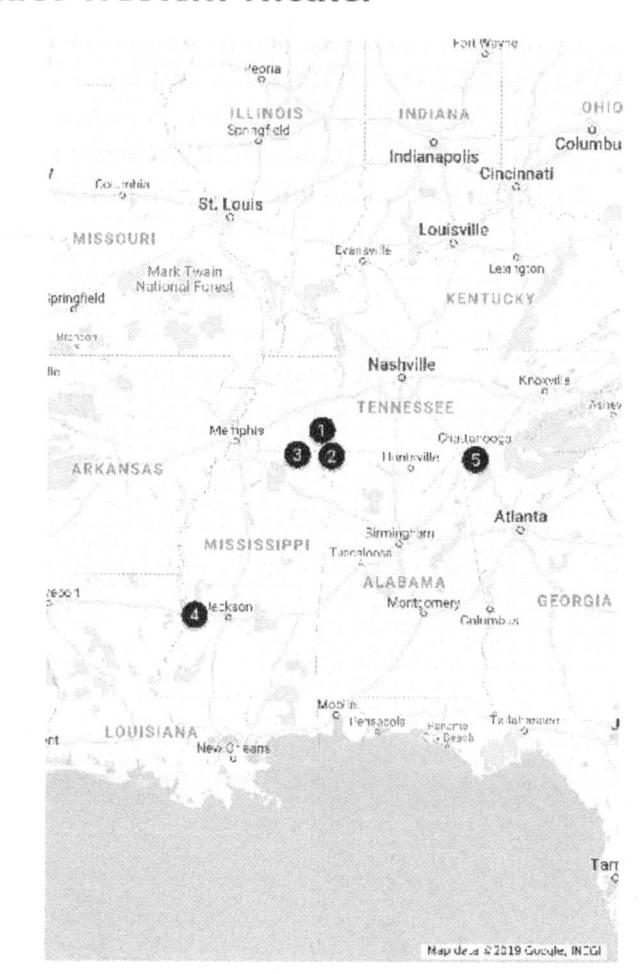

Untitled layer
- ① Battle of Shiloh, TN
- ② Farmington, MS
- ③ Corinth, MS
- ④ Vicksburg, MS
- ⑤ Chicamauga, GA

Civil War Battles Eastern Theater

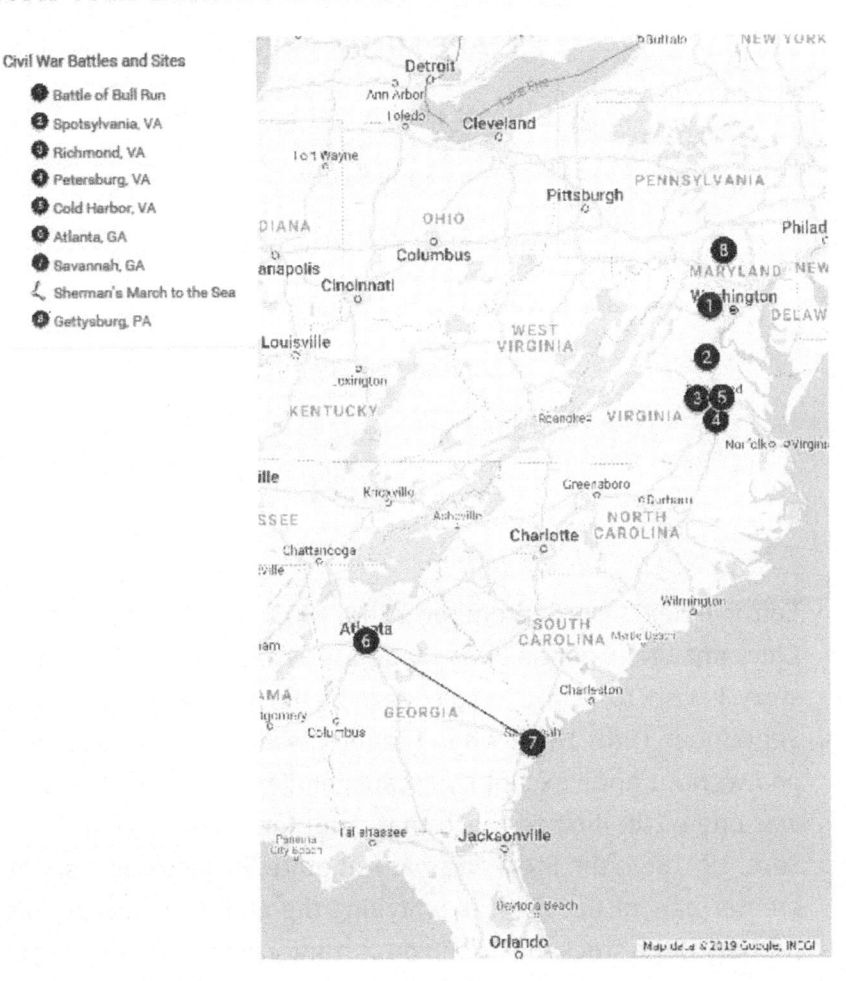

Civil War Battles and Sites
- Battle of Bull Run
- Spotsylvania, VA
- Richmond, VA
- Petersburg, VA
- Cold Harbor, VA
- Atlanta, GA
- Savannah, GA
- Sherman's March to the Sea
- Gettysburg, PA

ESCAPE FROM PRISON

And Subsequent Adventures in the

Sunny South

By James McHenry, M.D.,

Late private, Co. H, 22nd Ill. Vol. Infantry

(Copyright applied for.)

Chapter I

Editor Index: On September 20th, 1863 your correspondent, at Chickamauga, Georgia, was made a prisoner of war.[1] In my little story I wish to skip a whole year of horrors which brings us to September 19th, 1864, when I found myself still a prisoner of war, and without hope except by escape, and at Florence S.C. prison.[2] I was one of the first to reach that death pen, and at that time, viz. Sept. 19, 1864, the Stockade was not quite finished. So, I spent the greater part of the night in watching the guards at the unfinished portion of the stockade, for an opportunity of escape. Finding every avenue of escape guarded, in despair, ragged, starved and forlorn, I flung myself down and for a time forgot my misery and despair in the land of dreams. In the morning I was awakened by the clamor of the prisoners to be allowed to go for some rails that lay beyond the guard line, with which to cook their meal that had just been issued. When I reached the place, a number had been taken out by the guards, and I was informed by two sentinels that no more could pass. I called the attention of the guards that others were passing behind them, and when their attention was thus attracted, I sprang across the guard line, in what I thought my best time, better time than I ever made in running a race with anybody; but I had not made over two rods, when the guards discovered the trick and both turned and fired at me. The bullets had no other effect on me however, except as the poet Milton would have put it, "to add wings to my speed," and then I made such time as I could not now begin to. Having thus drawn the fire of the guards the others started, drawing the fire of the adjacent guards, the whole crowd started in a pell-mell race for liberty or wood, as the case of each individual seemed to require. Then the whole force of Rebels were turned loose upon the escaped prisoners. The noise seemed almost like a battle, and as a consequence, right here, many a poor soldier made his last leap for liberty. All this time your correspondent was rapidly traversing a bee line for the North Star, not however very intent on astronomical discoveries. I soon reached a swamp lying athwart my way. This was soon traversed without any apparent danger or difficulty, several comrades emerging from the swamp at the same time, and simultaneously on the other hand a body of armed rebels. Another gauntlet to run; well, this was the first anniversary of my capture, (Sept. 20th '64) and as I had started out to celebrate it, and as I was on my running weight, having eaten about a pint of dry meal the day previous and nothing that day, so

I took the risk. While running through a corn field I drew my day's rations, viz. two ears of corn. Soon after passing the corn field I began to hear the deep baying of the blood hounds. Upon the hearing of them, I betook myself to the heart of a jungle or cane brake swamp. This was about six or seven miles from the camp; here I ate my two ears of corn, and awaited the advent of the hounds by a tree that I could easily climb, but they did not come, they were on the track of some less fortunate poor fellow. Night soon came and spread his sable mantle over the scene, but the rebels patrolled the swamp. Two of them passed by me about a rod distant, and in the darkness one stumbled and fell, the other laughed at him, and as soon as he regained his feet he remarked that "he would like to find one of the (compound complimentary adjective) Yankees," whom he'd fix so they would "have no further trouble hunting him." At the time I was lying prone on the bosom of mother Earth; when lying down at that time, I was not nearly as tall as at present, yet I seemed just then very, very tall. However, they passed, and when later in the night I began to stir around. The object of my search was water, for I had not had a drink that day. The sky had been by this time obscured by clouds, and it was as dark as Egyptian midnight, walled in by black cats. I evidently traveled in a circle for I could not grope my way out of the swamp, and I began to think I must perish of thirst. I recollected that I was in the land of my fore fathers, that one of my great grandfathers was with Gen. Francis Marion[3] during the Revolutionary War, cavorting through this very swamp perhaps, yet these glorious recollections did not assuage my thirst, or make me relish the idea of going to the happy hunting grounds from such a place. An Irishman Pat had been in this country some time, afterward his sweetheart came, and when they met, she said to him, "Paddy, I brought yes over a little rule ould Irish whisky, would yes iver have a dhrop?" Paddy answered, "Do I hear an angel sing?" I quoted Pat while in this place and condition, upon hearing a band of negroes beginning a plaintive, melancholy and monotonous chant, that is said to be peculiar to the plantation negroes of the far south. I followed the sound, and it was to me as good as a pillar of fire, for it led me up out of the wilderness. By this time my thirst was intense. I dare not venture on the habitation of man, and I could find no water, so I traveled on and on until it was nearly daybreak when I suddenly came upon a beautiful clear stream. I had heard of people getting lost on the great Asiatic and American deserts, and as they were about perishing of thirst, found water, drunk too much and died; so, before drinking any, I waded into it and immersed myself for a few moments, then drank. It was like emerging from the confines of a Dantean or Miltonian Hades into the beautiful fields of Paradise.

One incident connected with my escape, and then I am done with that part of my story. There was a man in prison, a soldier, a very good looking man, in fact handsome; he so much resembled in personal appearance, your correspondent that his friends were constantly calling me by his name and my friends vice versa. We were constantly being mistaken for each other. On the day I made my escape he, poor fellow, was killed. Some of my friends who were detailed to bury those who were killed that day, found his body, buried it, and placed on a board over the grave, my name, Co., Regt. and date of death. Some of these friends got through our lines shortly afterward on a special exchange, consequently when I reached home, I had the pleasure of reading two very touching obituary notices, referring to my death. They had found out all of my virtues. Rather a rare experience to read one's own obituary.[4]

Shortly after drinking of the beautiful stream, day began to break and I found myself on the banks of a small river or stream. After crossing it I found a small bush over which ran a vine bearing a variety of grape called Muscadines. After eating these, I felt very much refreshed. I then skulked along in the bushes for some time, and came upon a field not wholly cleared, for near the center of it was several acres of timber and underbrush. In a corner of the field remote from the house I found a melon patch. I took what I could carry, and hid myself in the underbrush and ate my melons. This was another joyous event, for it reminded me so much of the joyous and innocent days of my early boyhood. After eating the melons, I carefully reconnoitered the position, and to my surprise and joy found in the edge of the clearing a large persimmon tree, heavily laden with ripe and luscious fruit. I soon filled my haversack and cap with the fruit, then repaired to my retreat and enjoyed the feast, then took a sleep. I had not slept long when I was startled by the sound of stealthily approaching footsteps. I carefully investigated the matter, and found it was only an escaped comrade. In those days I am sorry to admit I dearly loved a little fun, and could enjoy it a great deal better too, when it was at somebody else's expense. So I concealed myself and awaited his coming, until he was within easy ear shot, when I called out "halt dah!" The poor fellow stopped, turned pale, and begun to tremble, but when he saw I was only an escaped comrade, his joy can better be imagined than described.

I then inducted him into the mysteries of the melon patch and persimmon tree. We staid there until nightfall, then filled our haversacks at the persimmon tree, shook hands and parted, he to the northeast, to try to reach our forces on the coast, and I to the northwest to reach East Tennessee. I hope he reached his friends. I do not recollect his name, Co., or Regt. for a few days later I lost my memoranda which I had faithfully kept during my imprisonment, and with this book other valuable data were lost. I have now told the story of my escape from Florence, S.C. and a few of the immediately subsequent incidents of my attempted escape from the Confederacy. If this is kindly received, I may follow up with the incidents of the rest of my life in the sunny south. I might have begun a narrative with the date of my capture at Chickamauga, and told of horrors at Belle Isle, Libby, Danville, Va., Andersonville Ga., Charleston S.C., but this has been done by able authors, and I do not wish "to repeat a tale that has often been told."[5]

Chapter I End notes

1   McHenry was captured at the *Battle of Chickamauga* in northwestern Georgia in September of 1863. The second costliest battle of the Civil War (36,624 casualties), Chickamauga resulted in a Confederate victory that stopped the first advance of the Union Army into Georgia.

2 Starting in September 1864, The *Florence*, South Carolina prison camp operated for four months. During that time, 2,802 of its 12,000 prisoners died, a mortality rate exceeding that of the notorious *Andersonville* prison.

3 Known as the "Swamp Fox," *Francis Marion* was a military officer of the Continental Army who effectively conducted a campaign of guerrilla warfare against British and Loyalist forces in South Carolina during the American Revolutionary War.

4 McHenry's *home* was Sparta, Illinois, a small town located about 50 miles southeast of St. Louis, Missouri.

5   *Belle Isle* and *Libby* prisons were both located at *Richmond*, Virginia. Belle Isle was an eighty-acre island in the James River in close proximity to Libby Prison. Libby was a huge shipping supply and grocery warehouse confiscated by the Confederate government. *Andersonville*, located about 120 miles south of Atlanta, was one of the largest and most notorious of all Confederate prison camps. Of the 33,000 men imprisoned there in August 1864, almost 3,000 died that month. The *Charleston* prison received several hundred prisoners hastily transferred from Andersonville because of the threat posed by the penetration of Sherman's army deep into Georgia.

CHAPTER II

In my last I had just parted from my comrade. The following incidents may not be presented in their exact order of sequence, as I give them only from recollection. After leaving the rendezvous, I traveled in a northwest direction and through a large pine forest. Almost every day and night was cloudy, so I had need of all my woodcraft to tell in what direction I was travelling, not having a compass. The moss on the north side of oak trees and a knowledge that the topmost tuft of leaves of pine trees usually pointed east, had to serve in the place of a compass. So to prevent myself from travelling in a circle, I would first get my bearings as well as I could, then select three or four objects in a line as fast as I had reached the nearest object select another further on, beyond the last one. By this plan I had no fears of losing myself in forest or swamp, while there was light enough to select my objects. Of course in clear weather my course was directed by the position of the sun or stars. Before morning it began to rain, and after daylight I found a clearing, a corn field and fodder stack. When I awoke it was still raining. I was very chilly and it not night so I had to turn out, dodge around a few farms, and was again in another pine forest. Corn was my only food that day and the following night. Next day I was in a large pine forest until late in the afternoon, when I struck another corn field and supplied myself with commissary stores. By this time it made my poor jaws ache most terribly to masticate the corn. Just then I heard a man calling hogs. I reconnoitered and found that his hog pen was away from his house as much as forty rods in the forest, but contiguous to his corn field, that he was old and feeble and that I could if necessary overpower him, and that he was accompanied by a little child. I knew he was not calling me, but I felt wolfishly hungry, starving in fact, so I went to him fully intending if I discovered treachery, to render him helpless and escape. I was before him before he knew of my approach. He could not have been more startled if a host had appeared.

I told him a "plain unvarnished tale" for which I apologized by saying that my appearance and condition would give the lie to any other claim, that I wanted food, wished him to supply it, and not to betray me. He informed me that he was, and had been an ardent Union man himself, although he had a son drafted into the S.C. service and killed, also a son-in-law who was a rebel, who also had been killed, and their families as well as his own, were dependent on him for support. Under his pledge of concealment and protection, and my pledge that I would not betray him in case of my recapture afterward, I went with him to his house. His family consisted of his wife, son's wife, his son-in-law's wife their families and two daughters about 16 and 18 years of age. You cannot imagine the surprise and astonishment of the family upon their introduction to a "live Yankee." Although the family were above the ordinary degree of the intelligence of the country, I thought for a while that I would be subjected to a phrenological examination for the purpose of determining the locality of the proverbial "Yankee horns."

It was not long until a bountiful supper was spread for me. After supper I would have been perfectly happy, had it not been for a realization of the unpresentable condition of my attire, not having a change of garment in over a year. As the sequel will show, something of this was also passing in the minds of my entertainers. I will not attempt to further describe the hospitality of this family: only will say that my reception and entertainment was more like that bestowed upon a son or a brother unexpectedly returning from a distant land. I certainly would have remained under their care and protection, as they offered for some time, could I have done so without subjecting their lives and liberties to danger and their property to confiscation, as they were all good, and the girls very pretty. The old gentleman's name was Robert Owsley, he lived near the town of Society Hill in Chesterfield District, S.C.[6] About 11 o'clock, after thanking them, and bidding them all a kind farewell I left with the old gentleman who accompanied me two or three miles, so that I might avoid the town, and danger of recapture. After parting with him I traveled until daybreak. Feeling again the demands of hunger I began to explore the contents of my capacious haversack, which was quite heavy since I had left Mr. Owsley's. I found a bundle done up in a napkin. Undoing it, I found a bountiful breakfast; seated by a beautiful spring, it is unnecessary to say I enjoyed it. Upon taking up my haversack I found it heavy. Being surprised I investigated further, and found to my delight a full suit of under clothes, a pair of pants, an over shirt and a pair of socks. The clothing that I wore was the same in which I had been captured, and was so ragged that the least fastidious tramp the United States had turned out since the war, would have rejected them with disgust. So I took an old jack knife, dug a hole and buried the old clothes out of sight, for fear that if found, they might call down upon Mr. Owsley the suspicion of the rebs that he had furnished some poor fellow better clothes. But let us discuss this event as briefly as possible. It is a subject upon which I do not like to dwell, for I feel the pangs of a stricken conscience whenever I recall the event, and the amount of life there wantonly sacrificed. After taking a bath I donned the new clothing, which fit remarkably well. (I was not as hard to fit then as now), and felt that in appearance I was a little more at least, than an ordinary good looking Johnnie Reb. During the day the sun shone warmly, and finding a dry secluded spot and lay down and slept. My finger nails grew more that day than on any other since my capture, over a year previous. When I awoke I resumed my journey with quite an appetite, and found it rough to get down again to my ordinary corn diet. The night following I met with no incident worthy of relating, except that it constantly rained, and I had to keep moving or I would chill. About day break I ran onto a spring near a house, where a large washing hung on the bushes to dry. I saw a good vest and coat, homespun butternut, and I knew they would fit me. Then I thought of the tremblings and thunders of smoke-capped Sinai, where 'tis said emanated "Thou shalt not steal." I thought of my Sunday school lessons in early life, and of that beautiful little hymn beginning "It is a sin to steal a pin etc." Then I thought of the rule "Self preservation is the first law of nature", "necessity knows no law" then thought of the Great Reformer of Galilee and his disciples in the corn field on Sabbath, so I drew the coat, vest and a heavy bed comfort and emigrated from the locality. It had been raining nearly all night and was still raining, so I travelled until nearly sun down. By the time it had cleared up somewhat, impelled by hunger I approached a log cabin. Here I found two women one an aged woman and the other her daughter. They informed me that they were Union in sentiment, though they had a son and brother who unfortunately was a rebel, and was home on a furlough but had gone out to see his sweetheart, and might return at any moment. However if I would partake of their hospitality such as it was, I was welcome. The younger lady was a war widow, her husband having been killed in the Confederate service. She told me however to trust me and in her eye I read truth, then I partook of a meal that I thought a prince might relish, had he been in my condition. The younger mounted guard in the porch for the return of her rebel brother--whose sweetheart by the way was a rebel. After finishing my meal the elder lady built a fire, made a pallet in front of the fire and suggested that I lie down take a sleep, and dry my clothes.

I slept a short time, and when I awoke there was sitting near me a big burly butternut son of the south, heavily armed with revolvers and bowie knife. I sprang up in amazement at my situation, and supposed betrayed, when he coolly informed me that there was no cause of alarm on my part as he was also a Union man and perhaps suffered more than I for the cause of the Union. Both of the women stepped in and vouched for him and his sentiments, then resumed their watch for the return of the young rebel soldier. After a long chat with the stranger, in which I learned he was the young widow's sweetheart, and in which he tried to induce me to cast my lot with him and his comrades and await the advent of Sherman and his armies, which he considered the safer course. I stepped upon the porch and asked the young widow if it was possible to procure a chew of tobacco. To my surprise she pulled from her pocket a log plug and handed it to me. I could not have been more surprised had I been struck by a bullet from a rose bud. I took a chew, then handed it back, when she took a chew and handed it back to me with the request that I keep it, as she "had plenty."

By this time my clothing was dry and I felt comfortable. I returned to the room and had another chat with the stranger. Suddenly the young widow appeared with the startling intelligence that her brother and some company were coming. She took her bonnet, and led me from the rear of the cabin to an adjacent forest; her friend the stranger betook himself to a place of safety. When she and I were alone, she attempted to direct me so that I could cross by a foot bridge, a swamp that was now overflowed, and lay across my way. She was fearful however that I might lose my way, on account of the intricate nature of the paths and roads between there and the foot bridge. She then offered to conduct me to the foot bridge, and I gladly accepted her escort. Upon reaching the foot bridge, I thanked her for her kindness and bid her good bye.

Chapter II End notes

6   *Society Hill, South Carolina* is located about 23 miles north-northwest of Florence.

7 The Union army commanded by General *William Tecumseh Sherman* had captured Atlanta on September 2, 1864, eighteen days before McHenry's escape from the Florence prison. Sherman's "March to the Sea" commenced in mid-November, and his 60,000-man army arrived at Savannah, Georgia on December 21.

Chapter III

For the young widow and her mother spoken of in last chapter, I can cherish the most kindly recollections, and I am sorry that I have forgotten their names. I hope that she (the younger lady) and her sweetheart survived the war, married and happy, blessed with peace and plenty. The country through which I was traveling, seemed now to be a succession of hills and swamps. The hills were usually covered by a growth of pine trees, the swamps either canebrake or dense jungle with cypress and other trees. On next morning I had succeeded in crossing another swamp, ate a breakfast from my haversack, which had been filled at the house of the widow on the previous evening. I then started on a road through the forest that led over the next hill, in the direction I wished to go. It was now between daybreak and sunrise, and I had no expectation of meeting anyone so early in the morning. However in making a curve in the road, I was brought vis-à-vis with a rebel cavalry man, mounted and armed capable. There was no chance for escape so I determined to pass myself off for a rebel. He accosted me with a cheery "good morning." I answered his salutation, and asked him how he came to be so far from camp? He told me that he had received a furlough for a few days to recruit his health, and was on his way now to meet a few friends at a rendezvous, to have a deer hunt that day, and the next day he expected to return to camp. I begged his pardon for detaining him, wished him a merry hunt, and a good time with his friends, and started on. "But," said he, dropping his hand to a double barreled shot gun "hold on." I "held on"--and by an effort looked him in the face--ready to tell any lie that the exigencies of the case might seem to require, just like a boy who wishes to avoid a whipping. Said he "Where are you from?" I told him "from camp down at Florence." "What reg't do you belong to?" I named a reg't of S. Carolinians on duty at Florence. "Where are you going?" "Down to Chester district to take a rest and visit some friends," naming an uncle of my father who lived there at that time. He then looked at me intently for a moment, then said very deliberately, "Your tongue tells a very straight story, but you face says it's all a damned lie. You are one of the escaped prisoners from Florence." This satisfied me at once that I was not cut out for a George Washington, and that I had been spoiled one half in making. I could force my tongue to tell a very reputable lie, but could not force my face to corroborate it, so I asked him "if so, what then?" "Before I tell you, I want you to answer truthfully, a few more questions, and for your sake you had better tell the truth" said he. I told him it was all right, I would answer correctly, and to ask his questions. He then asked "are you an escaped prisoner?" I told him I was. "Very well," said he, "I almost knew it." "If I agree to tell you something to your benefit, will you pledge to me your honor as a soldier not to betray me, come what will?" I now began to be interested in the conversation, and readily gave the desired pledge. He then informed me that he was a Union man, and in that immediate vicinity he had two brothers and several friends hiding to avoid the draft, he said also that he would be with them if his health would permit of the necessary exposure, that the light nature required of him permitted him to take better care of his health than if he attempted to avoid the rebel service. He offered to take me to his house, conceal and feed me, and advised me to let him conduct me to his brothers and friends, and there await the coming of Sherman and his army. After I had with thanks declined his offer, and given him my reasons for doing so, he gave me some instructions relative to the topography and geography of the country, called me to him, emptied his haversack into mine, bid me good day and good speed, then we shook hands and parted.[8] Early in the afternoon of that day, I arrived at a stream that was very much swollen by the recent rains, and had overflowed its low swampy banks on both sides. I was then weary and foot sore, so I retraced my footsteps a short distance to where there were many dense pine tree tops. Their bodies had evidently been cut and hauled away for lumber. The clouds had by this time rolled away, and genial Sol smiled down, as I crawled into a pine tree top, and hid myself. I was soon wrapped in the embrace of Morpheus, and was travelling with Somnes in the land of dreams. That is, I went to sleep. I had probably slept more than an hour or two, when I was awakened by the sound of wood choppers near at hand. They were chopping the pine tops into firewood. The party consisted of several Negroes, accompanied by an overseer. How I did hope that they would not come to the one in which I lay concealed; vain hope! The very tree tops in which I was concealed, was pointed out by the overseer, and a party of the woodchoppers started for it. I was in for it now, so I stepped deliberately out in full view of the party, then turned and walked away toward the overflowed swamp. The party stopped as suddenly as if some frightful vision had arisen before them. I soon passed out of the sight and reached the swamp. I followed, now more rapidly, along its edge for some distance. The wood chopping party had with them some wagons. Their surprise did not last long, for soon I heard them rattling speedily over the hill, and from the time they were making I inferred that they "meant business," in which it was probable I would be sought as an objective party. I then gathered some long green pine leaves or "straw," and bound it to the soles of my feet. My object in doing this is explained in the following incident. At the prison at Andersonville, Georgia, as one the rebels suspected, that at a certain point the prisoners were tunneling under the stockade for the purpose of making their escape. To discover the locality of the tunnel, the rebels brought in a large squad of Negro slaves, who dug a ditch inside of the "dead line." While I was watching their work, one of them, unobserved by the overseer, said to me "Massa if you ever 'scapes from dis place, and dey gits after you wid de hounds, jes drap a little Kyan pepper in yor tracks, de hounds snuff it and can't follow you no mo', or tie to de soles of yo' feet some pine straw, and den dey can't follow you, sho'." Now he might as well have told me to put gold dust in my tracks as cayenne pepper, but the latter recommendation, if of use at all, was practicable, for in those regions, pine grew everywhere.

At this time I think the precaution was well taken. After I had bound the leaves on my feet, I think that I had not gone over a mile, when I heard hounds baying on my track. I then waded into the swamp, and upon reaching the creek, I found there was a swift current and I did not much like to undertake to cross it. I then waded up the stream on the bank of the creek, and found a tall fence built across the swamp. The creek was spanned by long poles or logs built into the fence. I attempted to cross over the stream on the topmost log, but when about the middle of the stream, it broke and I was precipitated into the deep swift current. I soon reached the surface and swam to a tree with thick foliage, climbed into it and went to roost. Here I unfortunately lost my bed quilt. The dogs, I judged by their racket, followed my track to where I had bound the pine "straw" to my feet, and there my pursuers evidently thought I had taken to the swamp, for I could hear the men and dogs in the swamp, as nearly as I could judge about a mile below me in the swamp. Night had somewhat advanced, and all was seemingly quiet, when I as quietly slipped from my perch, and waded through the water and jungle to the north shore. I then traveled in a North West direction until about midnight, when I struck what appeared to be a densely populated neighborhood. I did not like to cross it, for I might be captured by their "nigger patrols." I could not flank it, on the west or south westerly direction, but I found a road through the edge of a swamp that was not entirely overflowed, leading almost due north. This I took, so as to avoid the settlement. The ground here was boggy and trembled under foot. I had not proceeded far on this road until in the language of Sir Walter Scott:

> "At once there rose so wild a yell
>
> Within that dark and narrow dell
>
> As if all the fiends from heaven that fell,
>
> Had raised the banner cry of hell."

I need not say that I was startled. I took out my old jack knife, and cut a hickory club. I think it was a panther or some such specimen of the feline race. For a while I seriously debated in my mind the propriety of retracing my steps, and of attempting to make my way through the settlement, but I soon came to the conclusion that I would rather, just then, meet anything in the shape of beast that the swamp could turn out, than to meet an armed rebel, so I advanced. The quaking ground, the unearthly scream with its demoniacal reverberations, and the "darkness visible," all combined to make upon me a strange impression. I felt along my spinal region a peculiar thrill. I thought that I felt very much like our canine friends appear to do, when their spinal hirsute coverings assume an erect position--that is when they get their backs up. I thought of Hector[9] in Homer's Odyssic Hades when "hell trembled as he strode." I almost imagined that I was another Hector having taken passage with Charon, over Styx, and was now daring the denizens of Fiddlers Green. However when I reached the place from whence I thought the sound proceeded, it struck up again, but this time it seemed to be about a half a mile to the east of me, in the heart of the swamp. I retained my club, however, until I was past the settlement and out of the swamp.

I then travelled along in a North West direction as nearly as I could make out. I had found an old unused road that appeared to lie in the direction I wished to travel, and when day began to break, I sat down to rest on an old log that had fallen across the road.

I sat there but a short time when I heard behind me at the roadside, a rustling in the leaves. I looked and saw what seemed to be a small white object weaving from side to side. I thought at once that it was the animal that had so startled me during the night, and that it had been following me, and watching for a favorable opportunity for attack. It was yet so dark that I could not make out its shape. I thought the white object was a white spot in the animal's forehead, and as there was between it and me a bush, or sapling, I inferred that it was swaying from side to side, because it was hesitating on which side of the bush to spring. I now thought surely my time had come, but I instantly resolved that if I had to die, I would sell my life as dearly as possible.

I had no time to cut a club or even to get out my knife, so I picked up a heavy pine knot that lay at my feet, and hurled it at the animal with all the energy of despair. The animal was fairly hit by the knot; but oh! ah! whew! sho! Well, I had been mistaken in the kind of animal and its madus belli, or I would certainly have retired earlier in the action, and in better order, though not more precipitately, and left unharmed his memphitian majesty, in unmolested possession of the field. It was an animal sometimes called a skunk but with all due respect to our perfumers, I would suggest the name, as being more appropriate, of "essence vendors." At this time I cannot say that I was very elegantly perfumed, but can say I was most thoroughly perfumed. At least I may say that I would have preferred what a friend of mine, whom I take to be a relative of Mrs. Partington would call, "a little night blooming seriousness." Ah well! In the language of Shakespeare,

"The rose with any other name would smell as sweet."

Chapter III End notes

8   While a fugitive in northern South Carolina, McHenry encountered white southerners who offered him assistance. Opposed to succession and the Civil War, these *"Southern Unionists"* were usually concentrated in areas where slaves were not abundant.

9 In his epics the ancient Greek poet, *Homer*, describes the death of *Hector*, the prince of Troy, at the hands of Achilles, the greatest of all Greek warriors. Hector's soul is carried across the mythical river, *Styx*, by the ferryman, *Charon*. Styx divides the living world from the underworld of the dead, referred to as *Hades*.

Chapter IV

Soon after my last described encounter, day opened with a cold dreary rain. I crept between two fodder stacks, and slept. When I awoke I was chilled and hungry. I tried to eat corn, but my teeth and the muscles of my jaws rebelled. I began to feel very weak and my bones ached with cold. I left my hiding place to warm myself by exercise, so I again took to the woods. Early in the afternoon I came upon a cabin in the forest, surrounded by a small clearing. I ventured in at once, and asked for food. The woman said that I was "either a skulker, or an escaped Yankee, and that in either case she had nothing for me." Her principles were evidently proof against my good looks, neither did she seem to appreciate the peculiar brand of my memphitian perfume. Judging from her conversation and manners that my presence was an intrusion, I begged her pardon, gave her a Beau-Brumelian bow and withdrew. As I stepped out of the door, I saw a large dish of boiled sweet potatoes on a shelf outside of the cabin. These I turned into my haversack, and struck for the timber again. Upon reaching the timber, I again bound pine "straw" to the soles of my feet, then as rapidly widened the distance between me and that cabin. After travelling for some time, and not hearing pursuit, I sat down upon the hollow trunk of a large fallen tree, to enjoying potatoes. While thus engaged, I heard the sound of men and dogs approaching. Judging from the sound, it was evident that the men and dogs had several times crossed my track, and that the dogs either would not or could not follow it, so, as they approached me I slipped myself feet foremost into the hollow of the log, and thus concealed, I awaited my fate. The party consisting of two armed men and four dogs, passed within a few rods of my place of concealment, made quite a detour of the forest, and returned evidently disgusted. It was raining, and my place of concealment was dry, so I staid there until dark and had another short sleep. As soon as night set in, I set out. It seemed as if then I "loved darkness rather than light," but the canonical reason was not assignable in my case, at least from my political standpoint. This night was spent in travelling, and without further incident, until about day break when I found myself on a sort of peninsula reaching out into what appeared to be a large bayou or lake. As it appeared to be athwart my way, was in a large swamp, and there might be alligators, I thought best not to try and cross it. It was not yet light enough to see how to flank it, so I tried to find a place where I could improve my time in taking a sleep. The swamp was almost all overflowed, and to find a place to sleep this night might be difficult. At length I discovered a large pine tree, a regular old patriarch growing on the banks of the lagoon. I had discovered that where a pine tree grew in a swamp, that if it was of a large size, its annual shower of leaves usually raised the surface around its base several inches. The leaves do not appear to decay like other leaves, probably on account of the anti-zymotic and antiseptic qualities of the turpentine in the leaves, and a fire hardly ever penetrates a swamp to burn them, or wind to blow them away, so they accumulate until the surface is raised sometimes, some feet above the surrounding surface. I at once occupied this for a couch and it was soft and comparatively dry. The clouds had by this time passed away and I lay down and slept. I had a good refreshing sleep, and when I awoke the sun was shining, and his genial warmth had diffused itself through the swamp- but oh horrors! The little island around the old pine tree had changed to a literal mass of writhing snakes--water moccasins. One lay across my body, one across my legs, and still another across one of my arms. They seemed to have taken me for a brother of the Reptilian race, but I could not see why they made the mistake, for I was not a "copperhead."[10] Just now I can almost see a smile on your face kind reader, and almost hear the remark, "he had them bad," but now I wish hereby and hereon, to solemnly declare and affirm that at time I was a teetotaler.

Oh, yes it was a reality and to me a startling one. For some time I lay motionless, but gathering my senses and energy. I still held in my right hand a walking stick that I had cut the previous night. I suddenly sprang to my feet, laying about me with my stick in all directions, and such a scattering of snakes, I never before or since have seen. In an instant the island was cleared of them, except three or four whose backs I had broken. I then proceeded to crush the heads of them, thus illustrating the traditional enmity of the human and serpentine races, or rather the human part of it, for they had not attempted an attack on my heel, or any part of my anatomy. They had crawled out of the surrounding water to warm and sun themselves, after the sun had rose. On that day I encountered no further incident worthy of relating. I traveled all day in a pitch pine forest. Every tree was tapped and furnished with a trough, which was overflowing with crude turpentine. I supposed that the blockade of the southern ports had interfered with the export of resin and turpentine, and there being no home market for it the industry was abandoned. On this day I had nothing to eat at all. Night began with a cold dreary rain, and found me still in the forest. During the night I passed into what appeared to be a beautiful valley, but I was in such a streak of bad luck that I could not even find a cornfield to get an ear of corn. I was by this time hungry, starved in fact, weary and foot sore, and if I stopped but for a moment to rest, I would get cold and chilly. The rain continued, and my clothes were as wet as they could be. I struck a road that led me into a bend of a small river. On reaching the river it seemed to be very high and was a rushing torrent, and dangerous to cross, which was evidently the result of the recent rains. I followed the road down into the bend, hoping to find the bridge. I soon came to one, and beyond it a mill, and beyond the mill a large old fashioned residence. Instantly I resolved if possible to find ingress to the mill, and visions of meal bins passed before my mental vision, at which I was to satisfy the cravings of the terrible hunger that seemed to be gnawing at my vitals. I had not reached the center of the bridge however, when two very large dogs started down from the mill, baying fiercely and disputed my further passage over the bridge. They did not seem inclined to attack if I staid where I was or retreated, but a warning growl greeted me if I attempted to advance. I assumed my most dulcet tones and manner to try and conciliate their friendship. I said good dog! nice dog! but they were insensible to blandishments and impervious to flattery. Hoping that after all the stream might lie across my way, and that I might not be obliged to cross it at all, I retraced my steps until I was out of the bend, then followed up the stream for some distance, but it seemed to extend in a south west direction. It had now been raining steadily since darkness had set in. The ground and roads were muddy and sticky with clay. My clothing was saturated with water, and bespattered with mud and clay. I was now fatigued to utmost point of endurance, and almost starved and very sleepy. In this condition I lay down upon the bank of the stream under a small "post oak" tree and went to sleep. I had not slept long when I awoke thoroughly chilled. I attempted to rise but failed. In a second attempt I was more successful, for I assisted myself by catching on to the body of the tree, and thus pulling myself up. I had not made over a rod when down I went again. I believe at this time I would have given up the fight for life and liberty together, had it not been for a realizing sense of my unpresentable condition, and at that time I had a foolish ambition to be a good looking corpse when I died, and then I had strange repugnance to becoming food for the miller's hogs, so I rolled and crawled back to the tree again. I took with me a light stick for the purpose of using it for a walking cane to brace me. This I stuck in the ground near the tree, then after again pulling myself up by the tree, I stamped upon the ground and walked around for some time still holding on to the tree to keep from falling. This I did for the purpose of starting up my blood circulation, and limbering up my stiffened joints. To some extent I succeeded, then taking my stick to brace me, I started back for the bridge, fully determined to cross it or die in the attempt. The walk soon warmed me up considerably, and before I again reached the bridge, I cut a club. The exercise, and the anticipation of the expected fight with the dogs nerved me up and sent the blood tingling to my finger ends. When I reached the bridge and started across it, I held my club in one hand and my jack knife in the other. I walked over the bridge without interruption. I presume the dogs were asleep, but I was willing to let the mill and meal bins alone out of deference to the dogs or their kindness to me in letting me across the bridge unmolested. About this time the rain ceased, and the sky began to clear up, and there was a faint dawn in the east. I passed the mill and house, then climbed over a fence into a field, hoping to find some corn. Traveling in a northwesterly direction across the field, I came into a field of peanuts. They had been dug, and lay in piles over the ground. After eating some of them, I found it getting too light to finish my feast there, so I filled my pockets and haversack, and again plunged into an adjacent forest. About nine or ten o'clock the sun broke from behind the clouds and began to warm up things. I found a dense copse or underbrush, gathered together a lot of leaves, lay down upon them and slept until nearly sun down. When I awoke I finished my peanuts, rubbed the now dry mud from my clothes, and as the welcome shades of night began to creep over the earth, I set out for the northwest. This night was spent without adventure or food. Next morning was bright and I was hungry. I travelled on in hopes of finding something to replenish my commissary department. Suddenly I was startled by the laughter of some children--not much to startle a man--but I had to be cautious. I approached as nearly as possible to them, as I could without betraying my presence, and found that there were three or four little boys playing near a spring. Beyond them was a log cabin, beyond the cabin a hill covered by a beautiful grove of forest trees. I then went to the boys and told them I was on my way to Tennessee to see my folks, and wanted to get some food. The eldest, a bright looking lad in answer to my inquiries, told me that his folks were at church, it being Sunday, except his mother whom he thought would give me all I wished to eat. I went with him, but to my surprise he did not take me to the cabin, saying that his home was on the other side. We were now in full sight of a mansion with its southern accompaniment, a Negro villa. In the refined and elegant language of the period, "I had put my foot in it" at last. Not realizing this yet and willing to dare almost anything for food, I went to the house with him and he stated my wants to his mother, an elderly lady. She betrayed some excitement but informed me with a smile that was child-like and bland, that she would immediately order the cook to prepare me a meal. I did not like the appearance of things. In one corner on a lounge lay a coat, part of the uniform of a rebel Lieut. Col., in another place a saber. I stepped upon the veranda and saw little Negro boys running in every direction. I stepped back into the room I had just left, and my eyes sought in vain, every corner, nook and cranny for firearms, but none were in sight. I then visited the kitchen and saw that there was no preparations for a meal in progress. I felt that word was being sent to her own people, or to neighbors of the family of my presence. I then said to the old lady, that from appearances I judged that treachery, instead of food for me appeared to actuate her, and then I wished her a good day. I then passed into a lane where I met an elderly man who told me that I had better surrender to him, and he would treat me well and afterward turn me over to the military authorities. If I did not surrender, the consequences to me might be serious. I advised him to be careful how he used threats, that it might in the unsettled condition of the country prove dangerous. He spoke of the impossibility of my escape, that their hounds could track me down etc. I told him that I had no time to parley with him, that I had to go. At this time I saw a man coming up the lane, so I hurriedly bid him good day and started down the lane. The old gentleman, and the man I saw coming were unarmed, and I wished to create the impression that I was, so I walked very deliberately, yet with some haste until I had passed through the lane. The road then passed through a forest and along the edge of a swamp, the two men following at a respectful distance, about two hundred yards. When I reached the edge of the swamp, I turned upon my followers to give them a final "bluff." I hallooed back to them, "men, I do not relish being followed, but if you will follow further, perhaps you had better get your blood hounds, I am ready for them and you also." I then turned with the intention of plunging into the swamp, and as I turned I heard a voice in front of me call out, "surrender." I looked, and there was a Confederate officer, shielded by a tree about a rod distant, with a fine old fashioned hunting rifle, and he had a "bead" on my heart. I saw at once that he "meant business," so I said "it seems to me about the proper thing to do just now, as you are armed and I am not." "Hold up your hands," said he. The game was up, so up went my hands also. I was again a prisoner of war.--Interlude--a few maledictions, dedicated to luck, cut after the pattern of the "sailor's curses," then an acceptance of the situation.

Chapter IV End notes

10 The *water moccasin* is a venomous snake that inhabits mostly wet regions of the southeastern United States. Copperhead is a common term for another species of poisonous snake. In McHenry's time, *"Copperhead"* was also a slang term for a northerner who sympathized with the southern cause.

Chapter V

In my last, I was standing with my hands up before the muzzle of a rifle in the hands of a Confederate officer. I asked him why he wanted me to hold up my hands. He answered, "You said you were not armed. We will see." The two men who were following me now came up and at the suggestion of the Confederate officer, who still had the muzzle of his rifle pointed at my breast, searched me for weapons. I now asked the officer why he either did not take down his gun or end the scene by firing. "Have I not surrendered?" The two men who were searching me for weapons found my old jack knife, which had been so long a useful friend. This being all the weapon I had, the officer recovered and uncocked his rifle, stepped forward and offered his hand. As I gave him my hand, I remarked that I did so, "without hesitation or mental reservation, but had he allowed me the opportunity I would have very much preferred to have exhibited to him a pair of heels." I begged hard for the privilege of retaining my old knife, but was informed that it was an unsafe weapon in the hands of one who would take such desperate chances as I had done and they never returned it. I told them they were mistaken in the man, that I only took desperate chances when there were no other, that the most timid man on earth would prefer a desperate chance to certain death. After this, except the taking of my knife and that I was closely guarded, I was by them well and hospitably treated. After my re-capture the manner of treatment by the old lady to me was so different, that she seemed transformed into an angel of mercy. They had taken me back to the house that I had left. They all apologized for their "seeming harshness" urging the necessity in a military, of their course. They inquired of me my name, company, regiment, place and date of capture, escape and etc. Soon after reaching the house, the old gentleman disappeared for a short time and reappeared with a pitcher full of cider, and a decanter full of apple brandy, and I was invited to partake with them. As cider was not on my prescribed list of intoxicants, I drank of it heartily. From its effects I felt exhilarated. Oh how it loosened up my tongue! And how I talked to those rebels. As soon as we had returned, the old lady set herself earnestly to superintend the preparation of a meal. By this time several Confederate officers stepped in. As they called they were introduced to me. One was a brother of the old gentleman, the rest were all his sons including the lad, whom I had first met at the spring. The old gentleman, his brother and all his sons excepting the lad, I found were in the Confederate service, ranging in rank from a lieutenant to lieutenant colonel. At length supper was announced, and I was seated at their table with them, seven men and two ladies. I expressed my surprise that they should all be at home, and was informed that they had all procured at this time leaves of absence to attend a marriage of one of their number, the Lieut. Col. who had that day been married at church. He was a son of the old lady and gentleman. After supper I was informed that I was at liberty to take a stroll wherever I pleased, provided I was willing to accept the escort of two gentlemen.

I accepted the proposition and took a stroll my "body guard" accompanying. One had a double barreled shot gun, said to be charged with buck shot, the other was armed with a brace of navy revolvers. When we returned, the old gentleman re-appeared with more cider, of which I freely partook. After this I was subjected to quite a fusillade of cross questioning. This was followed by a running debate on the war, its causes, the south's "peculiar institutions" and etc. During all this time the Lieut. Col. was very dignified and did not condescend to engage in conversation with the "Yankee mudsill." I felt a little piqued at this, but the good food and the old gentleman's cider made me feel better physically and mentally than I had felt for many a day.

Robert Burns the Scottish bard and "noblest Roman of them all" once sang:

> "Lees on me drink! It gives us mair
>
> Than either school or college
>
> It kindles wit, it wankens lair,
>
> It pangs us fou' o' knowledge."[11]

So inspired, I suppose by the good food and the old gent's cider, I made an assault to break down the reserve and dignity of the Lieutenant Colonel. "So I am told, if my gallant son of thunder, so I mean Mars, if my theology is correct, was wounded by a dart from the bow of the little blind god, has gone and surrendered and re-enlisted, this time under a--shawl! Fell before the glances, shot from the eyes of a pretty little widow! Say my friend, how about serving two masters?" He then unbent his dignity and joined in a laugh at his expense. I will say that before venturing to fire this shaft at him, I had been in council with two of his brothers. He replied that he was happy to state that he and his wife were both good rebels, and therefore after all it was but one service. After this he joined in a conversation that lasted until midnight.

During the evening and next forenoon, several of their neighbors called to see the "live Yankee"--they called every northern man a Yankee. From the looks of some of them, it was quite evident that I might have fallen into the hands of less generous and chivalrous and generous foes. My captors treated me very kindly, and as far as they thought consistent with their supposed duty, tried to make me for the time forget I was yet a prisoner of war. Only one incident occurred to mar a kindly recollection of generous and chivalrous foes. It was this: one of them said, "from your conversation, language, and general knowledge of the positions of the armies, and subjects at issue, we must infer that you have not given us your real rank, or the nature of your service, but also for the same reasons we must presume you are a gentleman, and so will not press you further on that point."

Now all this was in one sense complimentary, but the inference was that I had lied in my story to them, I choked down my resentment--I had to--thanked them for that part of their remark that was expressive of their good opinion, but begged to assure them nevertheless, that my rank and service were correctly stated. I had good reason afterward to recall the fact of their doubt, in regard to my statements relative to my rank and service. The old lady had me a bed prepared to sleep in that night fit for a prince, which I declined to occupy, so I lay down on a mattress and slept while two of my captors kept constant guard over me. On next afternoon I bid adieu to all the family, excepting those who were to accompany me to where I was to be turned to the military authorities. The whole family joined in an invitation to me, to return and be their guest after the war was over, if I was so fortunate as to survive it, and it was their hope that I would. I was seated in a buggy beside the old gentleman and two of his sons on horseback rode behind.

One was armed with the shotgun, the other with the revolvers. I called them my body guard, and hoped, that if they wished to consult my preference they would on this occasion, wear blue uniforms. One of them answered, that I must excuse them this time, as they had not very recently captured any Federal supply train. A short ride brought us to a little town, which appeared to be a military training station. I have forgotten its name, but it was near Charlotte, N.C. Here I was turned over to the military authorities. Here the old gentleman handed me a well filled haversack and a package of delicacies, which he said was from the old lady.

> "Oh woman! In our hours of ease
>
> Uncertain, coy and hard to please
>
> And variable as the shade
>
> By the light quivering aspen made;
>
> When pain and anguish wring the brow,
>
> A ministering angel thou. [Walter Scott]

I am sorry that I have forgotten the names of these people. I think the family name was Williams, but I am not sure. Sometimes I think it was Stephens. I have told about them to my wife's mother who was born and raised in that locality.[12] All of her sons who were old enough served in the Union army, yet she says her maiden name was Williams, and think it probable that the men who re-captured me were her brothers and nephews. Here I was placed in a guard house, and so closely guarded that any attempt at escape, would have procured certain death. I found here three other re-captured prisoners, who had escaped from the same place and at the same time that I did. They were Iowans, but I have forgotten their names. We remained at this place about twenty-four hours. During our stay here we were called upon by a Lutheran clergyman, who proved very conclusively from the Holy Writ, the divinity of the institution of slavery, and by reason, the efficacy above all things, human and divine, as a promoter of Christian civilization and morality. I did not have much talk with him, for at this time--for a wonder--I did not take kindly to the cloth. Next day we were marched into Charlotte, put aboard a train of cars and sent to Salisbury, N.C. Now kind reader, please indulge me for a short time, for I wish to give right here a brief review of my experience in southern prisons, and a word of comment. On Belle Isle and in Camp Libby, as the prisoners were starved to the very verge of death. The winter of '63-4 was one of unusual severity. While in the "Smith" building of Camp Libby, the rebel prison authorities informed us that our authorities had sent us some clothing. In our building we were allowed the choice of an overcoat or blanket, I chose a blanket. This was the only clothing that I ever knew of, or heard of, being distributed to Union prisoners. From Camp Libby we were sent to Danville, VA.[13] The food here, while perhaps a little more in quantity was decidedly worse in quality than at Richmond prisons. At this place the writer contracted a bad cold or bronchial-pneumonia, coughed up and spit bloody and purulent mucus nearly all the winter, but managed to avoid death from starvation and exposure, by accepting for an extra ration, and more comfortable quarters, the position of waiter in the pest house adjoining our building, where the small pox cases were kept. This position was held by the writer for about a month, and during this time he enjoyed the most comfortable sleeping quarters, that he had while a prisoner in the south; viz. on a mattress with two small pox cases. One thing in connection with this is the strange fact that he never took the disease.

When I think of the horrible filth of those dens, to describe it without giving offence, would overtax the pen of the most erudite scholarship! The unsheltered and naked condition of those soldiers and the insufficient food. I often wonder that any are left to tell the tale. This leads me to think with a shudder of horror of the fiend Jefferson Davis,[14] who was more directly responsible for the treatment, condition and sufferings of the prisoners than any, and all others. After experiencing thus, the hell fire of his fiendish hate, and recollecting the sudden death of Gen. Taylor, and recollecting the rebuke Gen. Taylor administered to Davis on the field on Buena Vista, for the position in which those brave men, the "Mississippi Rifles" had been placed, I say when I think of these things, I cease to wonder at the mysterious fate of Gen. Taylor.

Jefferson Davis

President of The Confederate States of America

And then on the other hand, when we find that the Government failed to provide by special act for the few remaining wrecks of those prisons, patriotism and honor hang their heads in shame, and blush as they deplore the decay of Independent Americanism, and the advent of a generation of flunkies, plebian curs, who would rather pension such a man as Ulysses Grant,[15] who while president, would accept as a present from an office-seeking admirer anything "from a bull pup to a brown stone front." A man who exhibited himself all around the world, to draw a little flunky admiration, a "representative man of a nation? Whose rulers exercise their powers by the consent of the governed," who felt himself honored? By sitting down at theirs with kings and princes and other titular tomfooleries, who claim their right to rule their fellow men, was conferred upon them by the act of God in pouring over them a little hair oil! The man who said, "I'll fight it out on this line if it takes all summer." Then to make his silly words good, hurls his men to certain death, turns on the impregnable works of Lee[16] at Wilderness. Then chews his cigar and words, and does what he ought to have done before, uncovers and passes his flank, thus finding Lee behind his second line at Spotsylvania he again unnecessarily hurls his men time and again, to certain and senseless death, and is again forced to uncover and pass the enemy's flank, this time to find Lee in the "last ditch" at Cold Harbor, and again the same tale to tell, and when at length forced to flank the city, instead of quietly sitting down on Lee's communications, he butts his thick skull up against Petersburg. And in doing these things he manages to lose thousands upon thousands more men than Lee and his command. O yes, pension Grant. Give him a princely revenue--or a chance, and he will "salary grab" one for himself. Give him a little of the holy hair oil, I guess he would like that too-- but let the wrecks of those Hadean dens of death starve and rot with their helpless little ones, and care worn wives--but pension Grant, perhaps you had better pension Jeff Davis too, and have another object of flunky worship. Pardon me kind reader, my heart goes back to the graves of many a brave comrade and friend who starved and rotted in the dens of Richmond, Danville, Andersonville, Charleston, Florence and Salisbury.

And I must pause till it come back to me,--In March 1864, we were sent to Andersonville, Ga. My lungs improved somewhat during this trip, but scorbutus[17] began to develop itself, and by the time I escaped from Florence my system was fully saturated with the disease, and my teeth were all loose, hence my difficulties in trying to eat corn. When I escaped, I left my blanket at Florence. My clothes were in tatters, twelve days later I was again at this little town, and I had a good suit of clothes. A large proportion of my food had been such fruits as persimmons, grapes, muscadines, raw potatoes, melons and peanuts, so that when I was re-captured this time I found myself apparently free from scurvy, and although again a prisoner of war, I had very much bettered my condition and chances of life, by my escape.

Chapter V End notes

11   *Robert Burns* (1759-1796) was a renowned Scottish poet and songwriter. A farmer's son, he wrote poems and songs in the Scottish dialect that spoke to the common man. His most famous song is "Auld Lang Syne."

12   *Jane Williams Stewart, McHenry's mother-in-law*, was born in North Carolina in 1812. Widowed in 1857, Jane and four of her seven children, Amelia, James H., Minerva Elizabeth, and Sarah Jane moved to Ottawa County, Kansas. Jane died in 1888.

13   Located near the North Carolina border about 150 miles southwest of Richmond, the *Danville* prison consisted of six tobacco factory buildings. Life here for the prisoners was insufferable: smallpox raged, sanitation was nil, and the food was full of bugs, maggots and rat dung.

14   *Jefferson Davis* was the only president of the Confederate States from 1861 to 1865. During the War with Mexico (1846-1848), he was the commanding officer of the 1st *Mississippi Rifles* volunteer regiment and served with distinction when the American army defeated Mexican forces at the *Battle of Buena Vista*. His commanding officer was Major General *Zachary Taylor*, a national hero of the Mexican War and the 12th president of the United States. Taylor served as president for only 16 months, his term ending with his death in July 1850.

15 *Ulysses Grant* was the commanding general of the United States Army during the late years (1864-65) of the American Civil War and the 18th president of the United States (1869-1877). His presidential

administration was marred by widespread corruption and mismanagement.

General Ulysses S. Grant

16   *Robert E. Lee* was the highest ranking general of the Confederate States Army during the American Civil War. During a four-week period from May 5 through June 1, 1864, Grant's Army of the Potomac and Lee's Army of Northern Virginia clashed in several major battles including *Wilderness*, *Spotsylvania*, and *Cold Harbor*. During these three battles, the Union Army suffered 48,400 casualties while the Confederate total was 28,687. From June 9, 1864, to March 25, 1865, Grant's and Lee's armies fought a series of battles around *Petersburg*, Virginia, located 22 miles south of Richmond.

Confederate General Robert E. Lee

17   *Scorbutus* is scurvy, a disease caused by a deficiency of Vitamin C. Symptoms include spongy gums, loosening of the teeth, and a bleeding into the skin and mucous membranes.

Chapter VI

Arriving at Salisbury, instead of being placed in the military prison at once, we were kept for a day or two in a guard house at guard headquarters. In conversation with the guards, I learned that the prison was not yet used as a general camp for prisoners of war, but probably soon would be, and was now used as a prison for their own military offenders, also, to keep Union political prisoners and the hostages who were being held to be shot or hung by way of reprisal or retaliation. There was also another class of prisoners held there. They were men from the lowest haunts that reek with crime and infamy, in the purlieus of such cities as New York, Boston and Philadelphia. They were "bounty jumpers,"[18] thieves and murderers and in its fullest sense cowardly villains. The rebel general, Robert E. Lee had conceived the absurd idea, (strange in a man of his remarkable common sense!) that the greater part of the rank and file of the Union army were there by force, and wished only an opportunity to desert, but could not do so to the rear, so he promulgated a general order, which was well distributed in the Union army, inviting the Union soldiers to come to him, offering a bounty and free transportation to the "border." This caught the bounty jumpers and none else, and caused such a deluge on his commissariat, and the Confederacy of the most accursed villains that had ever been seen together before in the civilized world. Lee's communications with the border had been hopelessly cut, so that he could not send them there, and he soon found that if he left them loose, they would steal the Confederacy blind much quicker than the whole Union army could whip it, so he quietly gathered them up and distributed them through the various military prisons of the south, (strange in a man so generally credited with honesty!) He hoped to exchange them for rebel soldiers. Oh, why did he not shoot them all and thus earn the eternal gratitude of the north and south, and the world? But perhaps it is best that he did not, for then some of our highest official classes might have suffered, if not greatly in numbers at least in kind. At the guard house were confined several soldiers, mostly for petty offences, but there was one a Union man, who had absolutely refused to serve in the Rebel army. He had been drafted, and deserted. He was called "Joe," I have forgotten the rest of his name. Late one afternoon we--the Iowans, Joe and myself were ordered out by a rebel Lieut. to be sent to Raleigh. We were placed under the charge of a kind hearted old rebel Sergeant named Meade, who claimed to be a relative of our Gen. Meade. The Lieut. ordered Joe and me to be tied together. I protested against such an outrage and indignity on a prisoner of war. I offered my parole of honor not to attempt an escape in transit, if they would not tie me, but the Lieut. was inexorable. I quoted from Burns:

> "Losh man ha' mercy wi' your natch,
>
> Yer bodkins bald,
>
> I did na suffer half sa much,
>
> Fra a dady old."

He could not appreciate the Scottish bard. It was no use, so Sergt. Mead performed the operation, appearing all the while to enjoy it about as much as your humble servant used to enjoy a hazel rodding in that old log schoolhouse down in southern Illinois, when his heart only reached a little above the teacher's knee. Our arms were tied behind our backs and then we were tied together. At this time I did not know that Joe was not a rebel, so when the operation was complete, I said to him, eyeing the thongs with which we were bound, "Joe, from the color of your clothes I take you to be an enemy and that we have served in opposing armies, but for all that we can now profess a strong personal attachment." Quite a laugh from the rebels greeted my attempt at levity and Sergt. Meade begged of the Lieut. the privilege of accepting my parole, but he evidently thought, as has been the case with many other tyrannical idiots, that his power and importance must be felt to be appreciated, and so refused the request. So thus bound we were seated in a passenger couch and were soon being whirled away to the capital city of North Carolina.

It was sundown before we were started. Sergt. Meade was behind Joe and me, thinking everything secure, at length dropped into a quiet sleep. Then Joe gave me in a whispered voice, a history of his being drafted into the Confederate service, and of his escape or desertion. He said that he could have gone north, but had no acquaintance there, did not know how he would be received, and did not like to leave his home. He also told me that in dodging the rebels successfully for so long a time, he at length became careless and was captured. That they were taking him to Raleigh, there to be court martialed and shot, and now his only hope lay in escape. He told me also that if we could escape together, he could pilot me through to the north, and that we could sleep every day under a roof, comfortably and safely until we got through, and then I could find him friends and employment. All this was in accordance with my sentiments and wishes, so we at once began to prepare for an attempt to escape. We first succeeded in unbinding ourselves. Then Joe divided a heavy bundle that he carried, so that I could assume a part of its burden. This accomplished, we lay our plans. He sat next to the window of the car, and the window sash was held up by a forked key. We were to wait until the train would "slow up" in ascending a grade, and just as the speed of the train began to increase in descending the grade, so that it could not be easily or quickly stopped, we were to jump out of the window, he first and I next. Our plans thus being made, we sat in a constrained position as if still bound, awaiting the arrival of a favorable moment.

At length it arrived and each seized his bundle, Joe put his right foot on the window sill, his left hand on the window sash, made a spring and disappeared in the darkness like a flash, but he had so raised the sash, that the key which held it up turned, and the sash fell with a report like a rifle shot. I quickly raised the sash and made a similar spring, but the noise of the falling sash awakened Sergt. Meade in time, so that he caught me by the pants and pulled me back. This was my first great "pull back" and the probable origin of the style. I thought at least, Joe should have his bundle, so I attempted to throw it out the window. "Hold on" said Meade, grasping the bundle, "whose is that?" "Joe's" said I. "Where is Joe" asked

Meade. "Gone to where the yam vine twineth" I answered. Sergt. Meade remarked that he wished it had been me instead of Joe that had escaped, and would rather a "half a regiment of Yankees had escaped than that infernal traitor, spy and deserter, curse him!" "Let's see what is in his bundle" said Meade.

By this time Meade had taken a seat between me and the window. He and I then investigated the bundle and found a roast chicken, some turnover pies, biscuit and butter. After eating what we could of these, we found there was a suit of under clothes, a shirt and a pair of socks, also a large heavy coverlet made of homespun blanket on one side, and homespun jeans on the other and padded with cotton between. Now said Meade, "let me give you a little piece of advice, if anyone asks you again whose bundle this is, don't say, 'it's Joes', but say it's yours, for if they don't hang or shoot you down at Raleigh, you will be likely to need it this winter." It is unnecessary to say I profited by his advice. In due time we reached Raleigh and were taken into a camp in the suburbs of the city. Here I was at first confined alone in a tent and closely guarded for a day or two. In addition to the rations issued to us here, the ladies of the City came frequently and "hardly ever" empty handed. I felt that it might be said of me here, as was said of the Great Lawgiver of Galilee, when he was forty days in the wilderness "the angels ministered unto him." Most of the ladies I talked with here were Union in sentiment, and the rebel ladies lacked that bitterness and hate so characteristic of the ladies in some parts of the south, during our late war. In a few days I was called upon by a corporal and his guard, and was told by the corporal that I was wanted, so "I took up my bed and walked." I was conducted into a tent where were seated a number of confederate officers. I was afterward told that one of them was Col. Ex. Gov. Vance.[19] Here I was subjected to a rigid cross-examination by the officers. My name, nativity, regiment, company, date of capture and place of capture, history of imprisonment, date and history of escape, recapture etc. were subjects of close questioning. I could not see that I had anything to gain by concealment or evasion, so I answered their questions promptly. After they were through, my chief questioners turned to the others and asked, "what do you think gentlemen?" Then another asked me how I came to "be wearing that uniform?" I answered, "Well gentlemen, with me it's "Hobson's choice"[20] for since the date of my capture at Chickamauga, until I escaped at Florence, S.C. one year, I had not drawn any clothing, so you can easily imagine the condition of my wardrobe when I escaped. So leaving out of consideration the morality or propriety of the act, I drew this suit--from off some bushes where they had been hung to dry on wash day, as I was trying to emigrate North West." He then remarked to his associates that I told too straight a story to be a spy. My astonishment can scarcely be imagined! On trial for my life as a spy! Before a court martial, and never know it, or suspicion it until a verdict of acquittal is rendered! That is the nature of the service in which my late captors thought me engaged! Ah well! That is why Meade said I might need those things if "they did not hang or shoot me down at Raleigh." But now that danger is passed. Then I said, "Gentlemen, I presume I should thank you, but had I known that was what you wished to learn, I could have told you so at any time." I was then sent to the tent with the Iowans, and on next evening we were sent back to Salisbury. No incident worthy of record on our way back to this city. Arriving there before daylight, we were marched into the military prison at that place. Again "into the jaws of death, into the mouth of hell."

As to the fate of Joe, all that I could learn, was that they had not at that time re-captured him.

Chapter VI End notes

18 *Bounty Jumpers* were men who during the Civil War enlisted in the military service to get a bounty and then deserted. An act passed by the U.S. Congress in March 1863 stipulated that three-year enlistees received $300. The bounty system was exploited by many who enrolled, then deserted multiple times.

19 *Zebulon Baird Vance* was a Confederate military officer, governor of North Carolina (1862-1865, 1877-1879), and a U.S. senator (1879-1894).

Zebulon Baird Vance

20 *Hobson's Choice* is an apparently free choice when there is no real alternative. "Take it or leave it" exemplifies the nature of this "choice."

Chapter VII

When I again reached Salisbury the first rebel I met was my friend Sergt. Meade, who greeted me with--hello yank! They didn't hang you for a spy after all! He then gave me some information that served me a good turn. He told me that they "had some damned mean men in the confederacy," and that some of them had conspired to put the Iowans and me in with the deserters, so as to have us robbed of our food and clothing, after which we were to be placed in with and held as hostages. He told me also, that there was a man in the southeast corner of the room to which we were sent who answered to the name of "Illinois" who would stand by me. After this I had no opportunity of communication with the Iowans, so when we were turned into the large room with these scoundrels, the Iowans distributed themselves wherever they could find room to lie down. I sought the south east corner of the room and asked if there was anyone there answering to the name of "Illinois?" "Here I am, what's wanted?" said a rather fine looking young man, stepping to my side. I told him that Sergt. Meade had sent me to him for advice and friendship. Just then some of the scoundrels set up the howl so often heard, and told of at Andersonville, fresh fish! fresh fish! Just then the villains caught and stripped one of the Iowans of all his clothing, except what under clothing he had on, then caught him by the heels and dragged him up and down the room, which I think was about 100 or 120 feet long, until the poor fellow was more dead than alive, and all the time hurling at the poor fellow their villainous epithets. I had in my hands a club and wished to attack the scoundrels, but I was told could do no good just then and would probably provoke them to murder the Iowans and me also. Just then "Illinois" said "I know of another man who will stand by us." He left but soon returned with a man whom he called "Massachusetts." In a short time they had served the other two Iowans in a similar manner. By this time it was nearly sunrise, and I was so enraged that I believe that even had I been certain of death, I would have attacked the villains had it not been for my new found friends. After they were through with the Iowans one of their leaders called out, "here is another fresh fish up here," starting to where I was. My friend "Illinois" now told me to "talk to them and don't spare the Queen's English either, and perhaps that's all we'll have to do, but if you do have to fight, fight to kill." I then told them in a mild? sort of way unsupplemented by any unnecessary adjectives? that perhaps I was not so very fresh as they might think, that I had the pleasure of meeting a few of their kind at Andersonville, Ga. Then something after the style of the Irishman who wished someone "to tread on the tail of me coat." I marked a line across the floor with my club and intimated that if anyone had a desire to emigrate to their masters--his satanic majesty's hadean regions, I'd gladly furnish him with a pass. Just then Old Phoebus[21] glorious Son of Day, with beautiful light, was peeping o'er the orient hills, and glancing in at a window, revealed a cerulean circumambient atmosphere. "Illinois" followed with a little speech, more remarkable for force than elegance, in which he stated that I was his friend, and alluded to some former combat he had had with them. "Massachusetts" followed with a similar speech, and each drew a butcher knife to be ready for the fray.

Both of these latter speeches served greatly to increase and intensify the blueness of the surrounding air. Oh Eloquence! Thou child of Genius! How often thou has moved the world! How often thou hast burned with a brilliancy and beauty that has bewildered reason and thought, and led men to glory and death--and now supplemented by a "sprig of Shillalah"[22] and two butcher knives, thou causeth over a hundred desperate ruffianly villains to cower like whipped curs, before three men. Ah well! If I have to fight, that's the way I like to do it. A Confederate officer accompanied by Sergt. Meade now appeared upon the scene. The situation was quickly made known to Meade, who immediately told it to the officer. The officer then stepped forward and informed the ruffians that "not one mouthful of their rations would be issued to them until everything taken from the Iowans was returned." This was evidently a new game on them, for they sat sullen for an hour or two. At length finding the officer meant just what he said, they gave in. First a boot, then a shoe, then a bundle of clothes were thrown into the center of the room, and at length everything taken from the Iowans was given up and we were then marched out of that building into one used as quarters for the hostages. The building in which the described incidents took place, was formerly a large factory of some kind, and the largest building within the prison enclosure, and these scenes were enacted on the upper floor. Sergt. Meade and others informed me, that prior to this time it was no uncommon thing for these ruffianly villains to take prisoners who had been thrust among them for a night, and when they would attempt a resistance to these fiendish atrocities, these villains after robbing them would throw them out of the windows, and some they first murdered, and then threw them out. This story was fully corroborated by "Illinois" and "Massachusetts," both of whom bore scars to testify of deadly combats with the villains on behalf of poor helpless prisoners who had thus "fallen among thieves." After this I was not a little anxious to learn the history of my two benefactors "Illinois" and "Massachusetts." As during the day all classes of prisoners were allowed the liberty of the prison camp, I soon had an opportunity of talking to them. I was sorry to find that my friend "Illinois" had according to his own story, a rather disreputable record. He had enlisted in a company raised somewhere near Edwardsville, Ill. Early in the summer of 1861 the regiment of which I was a member, rendezvoused at Caseyville, Ill., on the O. & M. R.R. a few miles east of St. Louis, MO. At the same time his regiment was there, so we had met before. He mentioned names of several people in that locality that I knew. While at home on furlough, he had assisted in the organization of a cavalry company and was elected its captain. For some reason his company and regimental officers refused to allow him to be transferred to the company of which he was elected captain. He brooded over this injustice until he at length determined to desert to the enemy, which he did, and eventually became a major in the confederate service. Subsequently he became involved in a quarrel with a brother officer, and accepted a challenge to settle the matter by the code of honor? His opponent fell and he was now serving out the sentence of a court martial, repenting and thinking, "That of all sad words of tongue or pen, the saddest are--it might have been."

While I could not help thinking, "If parts allure thee, see how Bacon shined,

The Bright, the best, yet the meanest of mankind."[23]

If it a fault to love the memory of that man, I hereby acknowledge it, and plead guilty, and if I met him today I would give him my hand with my heart in it, and say to him, "With all thy faults I love thee still." The story of "Massachusetts" was different. On the field of the first Battle of Bull Run[24] he had fallen wounded and faint. He had been carried to a rebel hospital, and during the subsequent exchange of prisoners, he was hovering between life and death from his wounds. Recovering from his wounds and on the verge of exchange, he was taken sick of the smallpox and again could not be removed.

After recovery from this he several times escaped, but always was unfortunately recaptured. At length exchanges of prisoners were stopped, and here he was. I am sorry that I have forgotten his name. Thus we see:

> Full many a gem of purest ray serene,
>
> The dark unfathomed caves of ocean bear
>
> Full many a flower was born to blush unseen,
>
> And waste its sweetness on the desert air."[25]

The building occupied by the hostages was second in size within the prison enclosure. It like the large factory building was built of bricks. I think it was three stories high. There were several other brick buildings, two stories high. These buildings were soon occupied by a hospital organization, each building being a hospital ward. There were some wooden buildings which were occupied by citizen or political prisoners. The "stockade" consisted of a strong board fence about 12 feet high. On the outside of the fence and built against it was a platform or walk on which the guards paced their beats. In front of the main prison entrance, and within a square enclosed by the buildings, was quite a nice grove of oak trees. Behind the buildings, the fence enclosed several acres of adjacent ground. The soldiers held as hostages were of all ranks from a private down to a brigadier general, and all confined in one building. The rations issued here were more in quantity and better in quality, than in any other prison in which I had been confined. However, this did not last long, for in a few days the rebel convicts were all removed, as were also the officers in the hostage building, then the other hostages were turned out of the building as ordinary prisoners of war. On the same day when those two classes of prisoners were removed, a lot of prisoners from the army around Richmond and Petersburg were brought in. As soon as we ceased to be held as hostages, our food was again reduced to starvation quantities. Winter was coming on and we were now without shelter. There was still another escaped prisoner from Florence who had been brought in. He was an Ohioan and his name was Abner Aldrich, so the three Iowans, Aldrich and I sat about to organize a building squad of twelve men, to devise ways and means, and to put into execution plans to build us a shelter. When the squad was organized, it consisted of the three Iowans, Aldrich, a young man who had served as one of Gen. McCook's[26] scouts, who on account of a loss of one of his eyes by a wound, we dignified by the title that Gen. Ben Butler[27] will carry to his grave; we called him "Cock Eye;" a young man by the name of Charles Burton, I think, of the 21st Mass. Infantry, whom, if I recollect correctly, was commissioned, but had not been mustered at the date of his capture, as a second lieutenant; a young man by the name of Thomas Wagoner, a Sergt. in Burton's company and Reg't., with four others whose names I cannot recollect, and myself. We set to work immediately, and built against the end of one of the hospital wards, one of the two story brick buildings. Except a heavy forked stick and a ridge pole, mud was our only building material when our adobe house was finished, it was, when material and facilities are considered, a marvel of engineering skill. It is said by tradition, that when Noah was building the ark, he was the subject of a great deal of wit and jokes by his neighbors, but when the floods came the tune was changed, then they would have liked to have taken a steerage passage with him, but finding that impossible told him to "go to thunder with his old ark." Well, Noah was not subjected more than we to the wit and jokes of the camp, while we were building our adobe. "It seems as if you fellows are going to stay with Dixie;" "Love's labor lost;" "Not going to be exchanged, eh?" "what will we tell your folks at home?" were some of the remarks with which we were constantly assaulted while at work. Poor fellows! Deluded men! How easy it is for some people to believe anything they wish! Alas, that this is true! Why not grasp the truth, though even it be a hideous deformity! Knowing what is before us we then can meet our fate like men. Is it not better than to shut our eyes to truth, than imagine and believe a false and gilded hope? We said everything we could to induce them to follow our example, but alas! comparatively few did. The reason of this was that the rebels deliberately circulated all sorts of stories relative to an imminent exchange, thus deluding the prisoners with false hopes. Their object in this was to thus prevent desperate measures on the part of the prisoners, to regain their liberty. In this to a great extent they were successful, but it had also another effect, and that was to prevent them from making the necessary preparations to protect themselves from the inclemencies of the now rapidly approaching winter. Thus they were led on by delusive hopes until winter was upon them, and then they were too much weakened by exposure and starvation to make even an effort to save themselves, so they died by hundreds.

Through December 1864 and January to the 20th of February, 1865, I think the percent of mortality was greater than at any time in Andersonville.[28] Our adobe house proved to be an almost perfect protection from the inclemencies of the winter.

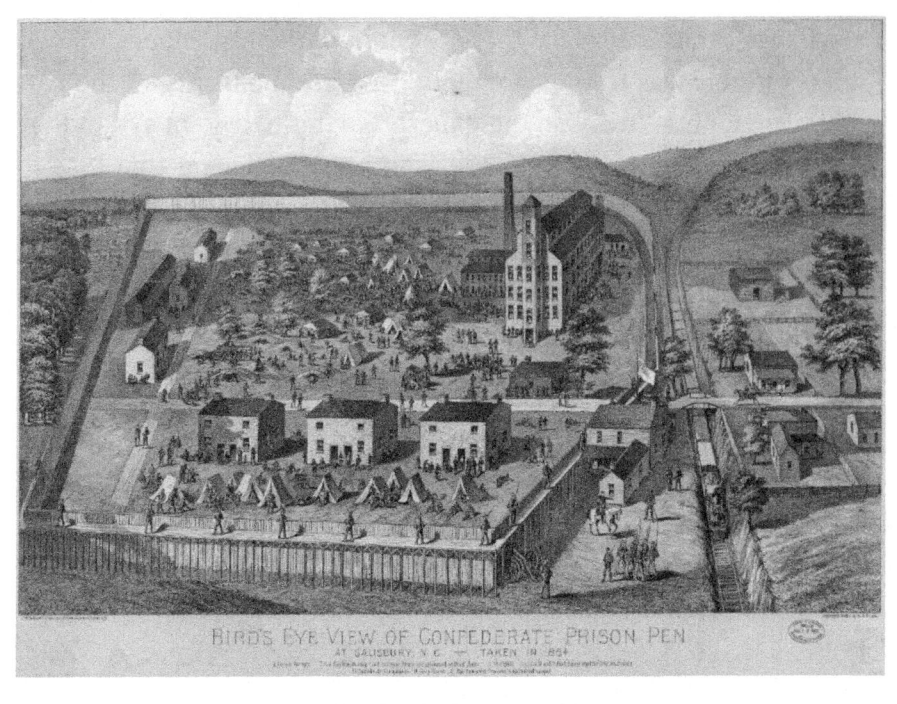

Lithograph of Salisbury POW Camp

Chapter VII End notes

21 *Phoebus* is the name for the sun personified. In ancient Greek mythology, Phoebus was Apollo the sun god.

22 *Sprig of shilalah* is an Irish term for a club cut from an oak tree. It also is a Saint Patrick's Day symbol.

23 *"If parts allure thee . . ."* These lines are from a poem by the great English author, Alexander Pope (1688-1744). "Bacon" refers to Sir Francis Bacon (1561-1625), who is credited with formulating the scientific method. Bacon was considered both brilliant and incredibly selfish.

24 The *First Battle of Bull Run* was the first major battle of the American Civil War.
On July 21, 1861, Confederate forces won a decisive victory on a battlefield 25 miles from Washington D.C.

25 *"Full many a gem of purest ray serene. . ."* McHenry quotes from Thomas Gray's poem, "Elegy Written in a Country Churchyard" (1751). This verse laments how the passage of time obscures the memory of what (or whom) deserves to be remembered.

26 *Alexander McDowell McCook* was a general in the Union Army and commander in the Army of the Cumberland. His troops suffered heavy losses at the Battle of Chickamauga where James McHenry was captured by Confederate forces.

27 General *Ben Butler* was a major general of the Union Army. After the war, he returned to Massachusetts where he became a colorful and controversial national political figure.

28 *Salisbury-Andersonville* comparison. McHenry's assessment is supported by historian James McPherson, author of *Battle Cry of Freedom: The Civil War Era*: "Measured by mortality statistics, Andersonville was not the worst southern prison. That dubious distinction belonged to Salisbury, North Carolina, where 34 percent (compared with Andersonville's 29 percent) of the total of 10,321 men incarcerated there died." (p. 297)

Burying the dead at Andersonville

ANDERSONVILLE PRISON
AS SEEN BY
JOHN L. RANSOM,
Author and Publisher of "ANDERSONVILLE DIARY, ESCAPE AND LIST OF THE DEAD."
WASHINGTON, D. C.

Prisoners at Andersonville

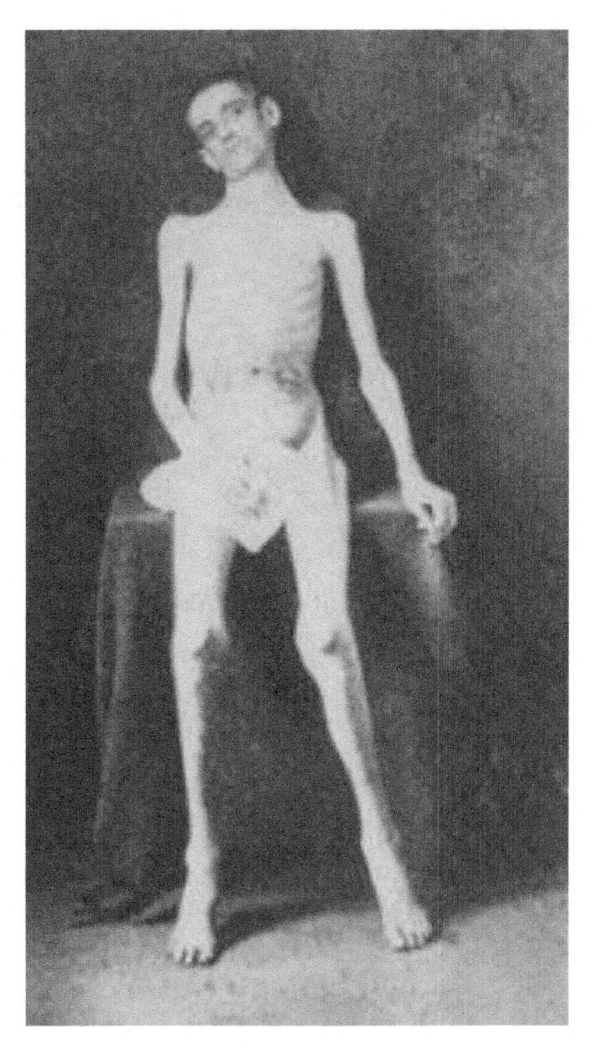

A survivor of Andersonville

Chapter VIII

Excepting two men "Illinois" and "Massachusetts," the first man in Salisbury with whom I became acquainted was a man of somewhat less than ordinary stature, but a glance at him told me that he was a man of more than ordinary mental and physical force, a man of energy, pluck and determination. A slight acquaintance only was necessary to reveal to me the fact that he was also noble hearted and true. In the expressive language of the old soldier "he had a heart as big as an ox." He enquired of me my history as a prisoner, and told me that he was not a soldier, but a newspaper man and that he had been captured while on a boat that had attempted to run a blockade at Vicksburg,[29] before the surrender of that city. I asked him, for what paper did he correspond? He told me the "New York Tribune." I asked his name and he told me it was Albert D. Richardson.[30] Now previous to this I had been almost a constant reader of the Tribune, and I told him so. I also told him that now he might be able, and at liberty to explain something to me had hitherto been a mystery. It was: immediately after the breaking out of the war, someone had corresponded with the Tribune from Charlestown, New Orleans, and other parts of the south. First who was it? And secondly, how was it accomplished? To my great surprise he informed me that I was talking to the author of those letters. He then told me in detail of the thrilling experiences and hair breadth escapes of which he was indeed the hero. He then invited me to his room, in one of the wooden buildings, and there introduced me to some gentlemen, one of whom was James Brown.

Of the latter gentleman I recall an incident. He had some books, and I requested the loan of one; with a decoction of "arf and arf" of affability and superciliousness he said, "with pleasure" and handed me a Greek work in the original tongue. I accepted with thanks the loan of the book, hoping to find some comrade who might be able to instruct me in that language by using it as a text book. Finding none I returned it to Mr. Brown.--It was all Greek to me. Mr. Brown was also a correspondent for a N.Y. daily paper, but I have forgotten which. Mr. Richardson while I was in took me to one side and told me that a few days previous he had sent down town and had made for himself a pair of boots, when they came he found they were too large for him, He asked me to try them on. I did and they were a perfect fit. "Now," said he "if you will wear them out for me, I will be under obligations to you." I said, "My dear sir you are too generous. But please allow me to consider myself the person under obligations." This is only one incident of that gentleman's kindness of heart. Never was there a man more indefatigable in his work while in prison there, to alleviate the sufferings of his fellow prisoners, to prevent sickness and suffering, cheer the sick and comfort the dying, it appeared to be his self-imposed task. Nearly all the prisoners thought he was a physician and addressed him as "doctor." He with Brown and several others eventually escaped and reached our lines. Subsequently Mr. Richardson published a book entitled "Field, Dungeon and Escape." I shall ever believe that in the tragic death of Mr. Richardson by the hand of McFarland, our country lost one of its noblest men.

Albert D. Richardson

Charles Burton, one of the twelve who helped to build our adobe house, I believe was just before his capture commissioned a Second Lieutenant, but had not yet been mustered as such, was of the 21st Massachusetts Infantry. He was a noble hearted, honest and honorable man.

Talk of times and places "that try men's souls!" In these prison pens, in less than a week sometimes, a man's soul would be laid so bare, that if it had any or many weaknesses, they would so plainly manifest themselves, the merest tyro in physiognomy could read them like an open book. Yet Charlie Burton had no faults, except that he was wild and full of fun--which of course was very bad. About the same might be said of Thom Magovern, except that his ancestors had more recently come from the bogs of Limerick, instead of from England in the Mayflower like Burtons. Another man from the Bay state, Charles Miller, a boot and shoe man from Boston, was a friend of Burtons. During the winter he nearly died of what the southern M.D.s called Dengue, or break bone fever, a kind of rheumatic fever, very severe and dangerous. Miller possessed great pluck and nerve which saved him. Abner Aldrich[31] was somewhat of a character. He was a Chickamauga prisoner, nervous and restless, and always full of plans for escape. He like myself had escaped from Florence, S.C. He was honorable, honest and courageous. Twice he escaped from Salisbury by personating a rebel sergeant, once he was captured and brought back. The last time he escaped he was not brought back and I have never learned his fate. He claimed to be one of a large family of that name, who belonged to the Church of the Latter Day Saints, usually known as Mormons, who not crediting to any great extent, the revelation of God to Brigham Young of the doctrines of polygamy, left Utah for their old home in Ohio. I hope he reached friends and is well and happy. The three Iowans all escaped. One was brought back, but the fate of the others I have never learned. On the account of the condition of my lungs, and the precarious condition of my health generally, I made but one attempt to escape this winter, which I did by walking off from a detail to carry wood, playing myself for a rebel, but the fraud was detected before I had gotten clear of the rebel camp, and I was returned the same day.

An Illinois soldier, an Irishman, who claimed to be an ex-policeman from Peoria, Illinois, by the name of Thomas Dunn, was brought into camp one day, and as there was a vacancy at that time in our adobe, we took him in. At another time a portion of the 1st N.C. Union

Regiment was captured and brought in. As a mark of contempt, for a southern man who would serve in the Union army, the rebels turned their officers in with the "common soldiers." One of the officers, a captain, was also a Methodist preacher. Now, I am not much of a Methodist, perhaps not much of anything, especially in a religious, or Christian sense, so it seems to me strange that I find among the Methodist clergymen (and it has always been so) some of my best and truest personal friends. This Reverend Captain's name was Murphy. When I first met him he was, in one respect at least, like his master; "he had not where to lay his head." So after a council of our squad we invited him to accept of our shelter. For some time after we took him in with us he preached, but finding it impossible to evangelize any portion of a starving camp he soon gave it up and devoted his time to better purposes, i.e. to acts of kindness and words of encouragement to the poor suffering soldiers. It is said that "evil communications corrupt good manners," and I suppose this was no exception to the rule. At first we were a little afraid of his combined clerical and official dignity, but it was not very long until he became in a sort of dignified way "one of the boys," and could sing a song, tell a joke or story with the best of us, and for that matter could take a joke gracefully enough--if he had to. I recall one of his stories. It was of Parson Brownlow,[32] the great political, editorial and clerical comet that blazed across the Southern sky. "One day the Parson was going to fill an appointment to preach in a new part of the circuit which he never before had visited. The place was in a mountainous region near the line between East Tennessee and North Carolina. After travelling on a winding road up a mountain for some time the Parson at length arrived at a piece of table land, on which was a clearing and a log cabin. The surrounding country was wild, rugged and broken. Riding up in front of the cabin he called out 'hellow!' A woman standing near the door answered, 'helhi!' The Parson then said, 'Good morning, madam; I seem to be lost, can you tell me who I am and where I am going?' She answered, 'Yes, you are Parson Brownlow, and going to hell as fast as you can.' The Parson raised up in his stirrups and deliberately surveyed with his eyes the surrounding scenery. Then looking the woman in the eye, said, 'Madam, if that is true, I may judge by the appearance of the surrounding country round here, as well as by the appearance of the inhabitants that I must be very near my destination.' The woman acknowledged herself beaten, invited the Parson to stop and have something to eat, and afterward joined his church." Such was one of the Reverend Captain's stories.

Major Gee[33] was the prison commandant. Of him it may be said, that physically he was a splendid looking man.

> "You're the figure, 'tis true.
>
> E'en your foes must allue.
>
> But you friends they dare grant ye na mair."

He had not the slavish, hang-dog servile look of Wirz, but had always a "smile that was child-like and bland," and could confiscate 25 to 50 percent of the miserable pittance of rations allowed the prisoners, and sell it to men that had money, with the same grace that Beau Brummel or Lord Chesterfield[34] could ask the hand of a lady for a quadrille. If Wirz starved the prisoners, it was to punish the prisoners and save for the Confederacy. If at Salisbury, under Major Gee, a man had money, he could negotiate for an escape, and many escaped in that way. All the money that Andersonville could have held, could not have bought of Wirz for one prisoner his liberty. Wirz was a faithful, whining, cringing bloodhound, true to his infamous master. Gee was a sleek, pet-purring panther. Treacherous and true to nobody. If I now sought these men, I would hunt for the one in hell, for the other in Congress.

During the winter previous at Danville, Va., I had a comrade of Co. B, a Switzer, named John Baker. John was a carver, and by the way quite an artist. A little Jew, I have forgotten his name, but a major in the Confederate service, was on invalid duty and over the prisoners for a short time at Danville. By some means this little major saw some specimens of John's handiwork in the way of making pipes, so every few days he would come in and bring John a laurel root, and hire him to make a pipe, and by this means I became acquainted with the little Confederate major. Shortly after this the little major's health being restored he was sent to the front, and I never expected to see him again, but one day at Salisbury I saw him coming toward me. He had on then the uniform of a Confederate Lieutenant Colonel, and one of his arms in a sling. He was just beginning to convalesce from the effects of some wounds he had received in action, one of which broke an arm. As soon as he saw me he recognized me. Extending his hand he said "Hello! How are you? Vere is Sohn Baker, I vants anudder pipe." I told him John was not here, and asked him of John's pipes. "Vere not all wool unt a yard wide," he said, "they vas goot."

After some conversation in which he seemed to evince a sympathy for me in my condition and sufferings, I asked him if he could not on account of our personal friendship secure me a position on the outside of the prison, where by giving my parole of honor, not to attempt escape. I could enjoy a little more liberty and better food, and employ myself in cutting wood or cooking for the prisoners. He said he thought he could, and perhaps get me a better position than these. A few days later he re-appeared, his face beaming with pleasure. He seemed to think he had me now under eternal obligation to him. He told me that he had been successful, he could get me a majorship in the Confederate service. He explained that all recruits from the prisons were allowed the same rank they occupied in the Union service. I told him I was but a private. "But," said he, "you must claim to haf pin a major, unt I haf all the palance fixed." He told me I would get a commission sure. I told him that if that was all the way to get out now, I'd prefer to stay there until I would die and rot, then when spring time and maggots would come they might draw me out through the cracks between the boards of the fence. I saw him frequently afterward, but he never spoke to me again.

Chapter VIII End notes

29   *Vicksburg*, Mississippi was the last major Confederate stronghold on the Mississippi River. When on July 4, 1863, it fell to Union forces commanded by Ulysses Grant, the states of Arkansas, Louisiana, and Texas were cut off from the rest of the Confederate States.

30   A Union spy and famous writer for the *New York Tribune*, *Albert D. Richardson* and his fellow reporter, *Junius Henri Browne*, were captured and incarcerated for over 20 months in seven different Confederate prisons. These men escaped from Salisbury in December 1864 and found their way back to the Union lines. In 1869, Richardson was murdered by a jealous husband, Daniel McFarland.

31   *Abner Aldrich* survived the war and died in 1893 at the age of 50.

32   *William Gannaway "Parson" Brownlow* was an outspoken Tennessee newspaperman, author, politician, and Methodist clergyman. As governor of Tennessee (1865-1869), Brownlow promoted the Radical Republican agenda, thereby gaining the enmity of ex Confederate politicians and military officers.

William "Parson" Brownlow

33   *Major John H. Gee* was the commanding officer at the Confederate prison at Salisbury, and *Henry Wirz* commanded at Andersonville. After the war, both men were prosecuted for war crimes. Gee was acquitted of all charges while Wirz was convicted of conspiracy and murder and executed by hanging.

Henry Wirz, Commandant of Andersonville

Major John Gee, Salisbury

34   *Beau Brummel* (1778-1840) and *Lord Chesterfield* (1674-1773) were British aristocrats renowned for their social graces and fashionable clothing. A popular dance in the late 1700s and throughout the 1800s, a *quadrille* was performed by four couples in a rectangular formation.

Chapter IX

When the first prisoners were brought in, at the time we were turned out of our hostage quarters, we were ordered to fall into ranks with them to be organized into divisions and messes, so as to facilitate the receiving and distribution of rations. This organization was effected within the prison enclosure, a new experience for me, in the Confederacy, for at all other places, this organization into divisions and messes was accomplished outside the prison enclosure. Now I felt sure I must starve to death on the meager rations issued if I could not procure something more. I thought of the acorns growing on the trees, but this industry would soon be overcrowded, and would not last. Just then a thought came to me. I would watch to see if they would organize the next prisoners inside. So I went to the gate and had not waited long until a new lot of prisoners were brought in. They were marched in to where I was standing, and halted. The process of organization for rations commenced, and a Confederate officer mistaking me for a new prisoner, ordered me into the ranks. I stepped into ranks and when asked my name said Richard Jones. "Co. and regiment?" demanded the officer. I promptly lied, by naming the Company letter of a Massachusetts regiment. We were then marched to an unoccupied portion of the camp and there as "Dick Jones" received an extra ration. Dick Jones was the name of a friend of mine, a soldier boy from Chester, Illinois. I believe I was the first man in the camp that played that "Yankee" trick on the rebels. If so "I guess" that my new associations had something to do with it, and so I "out Heroded

Herod" that time. I will mention here that at the other prisons, a trick like this was impossible, one could answer to only one name, because at the roll call all were required to stand in ranks, or lie in ranks if they were not able to stand, until the whole camp had been called, but here a few of the divisions were counted at once, then were dismissed, so that it was possible to be counted in several places. I kept up my dodging into the ranks with new prisoners, until at length I was drawing from the rebels fifteen extra rations and answering to as many different names. It was not long however until many of the others "tumbled to the racket" and at one time there was about 3000 extra rations drawn. My rations that I could not eat I sold or gave away. One ration of bread alone readily sold for one dollar Confederate money. The rebels learned that such a thing existed, and undertook to cut off the "flankers" as we were called, and only partially succeeded. To accomplish this they drove all the prisoners off the square, and behind the buildings, then placed guards between the buildings and hospital wards, then had all the prisoners march into the square passing between the officers. By this means they caught nearly all the "flankers" for by this stratagem no one was counted into the square but once. The steward of the ward against which our adobe was built I was acquainted with. He was a Chickamauga prisoner and I think a Michigander. His name was Merrill. One of the back windows of his ward was open, and the door of the ward within the square, and so soon as I was counted into the square, I stepped into the hospital ward, jumped out of the back window and rejoined the procession in another division and again passed muster Jones, McKee, Hart, Smith, or any of my numerous aliases. I think the rebels succeeded in cutting off about 1000 rations this time. Of course I am lucky if I approximate the numbers as I can only give my somewhat vague recollection of these numbers. Soon after the escape of A.D. Richardson and his comrades there occurred one of the strangest and saddest episodes of prison life in the south that occurred during the war. An organization of the prisoners for self-protection had been effected. To a certain extent this was a secret organization and was rendered necessary by the inroads of an organized band of ruffians, scoundrels, and thieves, many of whom were our old acquaintances the bounty jumpers and deserters, whose raids were among the unorganized and helpless soldiers. With the consent of the rebel authorities, as at Andersonville, this organization of the prisoners took charge of the punishment of crimes committed within the prison. Among the band of the ruffians were two leaders whose names I think were Howard, a New Hampshire man, and an Irishman named Turner. Under the leadership of these men robbery, theft and murder in the camp became common. A court was organized, several men were tried and punished by the court, and the two men Howard and Turner were tried and were sentenced to be hung for murder. The organization and its court were similar to the organization and court that hung the murderers at Andersonville. Like Wirz at Andersonville, Major Gee agreed to keep the culprits secure, and deliver them to the executioners on the day fixed for the execution. But unlike Wirz, he failed to keep his word. Through treachery or carelessness he allowed the prisoners to escape. The trial and sentence of these men, and punishment of some of their confederates however, had the effect of stopping all lawlessness, theft and ruffianism in camp. After accomplishing this object the leaders of the regulators, resolved in secret conclave to organize the prisoners, or at least those of them who could be trusted, into an army. This was done and each one taken into the organization was not only sworn into the service, but sworn to secrecy. Each member was known to each other, by certain signs, passwords and badges, such as two pins or threads crossed on the lapel of the coat, blouse or vest. A brigade was thus organized, every company and regiment of which was thoroughly organized. The object of this organization was to be ready to take advantage of any opportunity that might arise, to make an organized effort to escape. At one time we thought our opportunity had come, but as the sequel will show we were sadly mistaken. We had learned that there was an armory, and ammunition magazine in town, and its locality. There was several pieces of artillery in town two of which were grinning at us through holes in "stockade." According to our plans, these we were to capture and take along. We were to get as many horses as we could find, mount the cavalry and send out scouts and couriers by every pathway and road, to try to get word to our forces to meet us with help, and we were to impress all the wagons and ambulances for the sick and wounded, then start for Knoxville, Tennessee. Such is a brief outline of the organization, its objects and adopted plans. These are what despair and death lent to us, in the many days of our living death. One day we learned from some prisoners just brought in that a large force of Negro cavalry were raiding in south of Danville, VA, toward Salisbury. A regiment of veteran N.C. Infantry who were on duty guarding us, we learned were to be called out to meet the raiders. In due time the N.C. troops were relieved, and so we all thought that now was our time to strike for liberty. Immediately a council was held and a time was set to make the break. The time of the old guard lacked a half hour of being out when they were relieved, and we all supposed that the new guard would stand the unexpired one half hour of the old guard and their own two hours. So the time set to make the break was 2 1/2 hours after the old guard were relieved. By this time it was thought that the regiment of North Carolinians would be far on their way, and that we would sever telegraphic communications between the town and all troops by cutting the wires. The train that was to have borne them away was due thirty minutes after the old guard was relieved, but was unfortunately detained by an accident, about two hours.

There were, up to this date, kept in the prison, eight or ten sentries, and the attack was so planned that the guards must be disarmed while they were being relieved, so that there would be the sergeant's gun more than double the number of guns, than were sentry posts within the prison. These arrangements were hastily made after the relief of the guard. A "captain" with a picked Company were duly posted to overpower and take the arms of the guard and relief, a company each to capture the cannons, one company to break down a side gate, and four companies with the assistance of those who had armed themselves, to force the main entrance, rush for the guns of the guard, arm themselves, capture the armory and ammunition magazine and arm the soldiers. The attack being planned for a certain hour, at which time it was expected the guard would be relieved, the surprise of everybody except the "captain" whose duty it was to disarm the guards, was complete, when it was found that the guard was relieved thirty minutes before the agreed time to make the attack. This captain when he saw the guard being relieved thought the time agreed upon had come, pulled off his cap, waved it over his head and shouted in thunder tones, "Now men, for liberty!" Instantly the guards were disarmed. Two or three of them resisted in surrendering their weapons and were killed. It lacked thirty minutes to the time and none of the rest of us were ready. I was in my adobe and had just finished rolling up my coverlet, and was filling up my haversack with corn bread and the precipitate attack fell upon me as upon all the rest like a thunder clap from a clear sky.

In an instant I was fearful that all was lost, but thought the men might be rallied, each company to its assigned duty. This might have been done had it not been for the fact that the N.C. veteran regiment that we thought were miles away, were lying about a hundred yards away. The men who had disarmed the guard began firing at the guards around the "Stockade," almost all of whom left their posts and fled. These were nearly all old men or boys who had been drafted into this service. Before the prisoners could rally or take advantage of the temporary excitement and panic of the rebels, the N.C veteran regiment began to mount the sentry beat in every direction and opened on us a terrible death dealing fire, and to add to the horror of the situation, the cannon began to belch forth into us grape, canister shrapnel, etc. The guards were rallied and also opened fire. Citizens piled up with all sorts of weapons and opened, adding to the holocaust of death. There is one step from the sublime to the ridiculous. One of the prisoners had sought and obtained permission to climb a tree, one of the tallest oaks, and cut off a dead limb for fuel. Not knowing of the contemplated outbreak, he was sitting up in the tree top, with an old table knife and a piece of iron hammering away at a limb. Some rebel thinking he was there to give signals, shot him dead. As he fell he appeared to turn over two or three times before he struck the ground. An Irishman standing near me exclaimed, "howly mither o' Moses! Wasn't it a domed fule who shot 'im? He might ave known the fall 'ud 'ave kilt him intirely!" The prisoners were falling in every direction around me, and the groans of the dying and wounded were terrible. We were at the mercy of a supposed implacable foe and had given them cause to open of us and so had but little hope of mercy. I turned to seek shelter in our adobe house when a young man came running up to speak to me, he stopped at the corner of our adobe but he never spoke. He was shot through the heart. He fell with his face in a ditch that was partially filled with water and filthy camp garbage. I lifted him out and found he was dead. I turned again to answer another man who came up at the other corner of the adobe when he also fell shot through the thigh. I carried him into an adjoining hospital ward, then I entered the adobe and for a while lay down so as to avoid the missiles. The firing continued and I began to think that the rebels meant to exterminate the camp, and if so, and I with the rest had to perish, I had better take my fate like a man, in testing the matter. So taking an old white rag in my hand I stepped out of the adobe waving it and shouted "we surrender!" "We surrender!" Looking over the camp I saw many others doing the same thing and in a moment shouts of "we surrender" went up from hundreds of throats all over camp. Then the firing gradually ceased. At the time, we were told that the rebels had four or five killed including a line officer of the

N.C. veteran regiment but they had ample vengeance for next morning there were between thirty and forty in the dead house who had been instantly killed or had died of wounds during the night, besides a large number of wounded in hospital many of whom afterward died of their wounds. I must state here that the number of killed and wounded at this time has escaped my memory, and I only approximate the number. On examination of the camp after the firing ceased, it seemed a miracle that out of the thousands of prisoners that so few comparatively were killed and wounded. Just as the firing ceased, a handsome, bright young fellow, perhaps about 17 to 19 years old, came up to me with blood on his head and forehead, his cap in one hand and a penknife in the other and said, "say friend, will you cut this bullet out?" I took his knife and cut out the "bullet" which proved to be a buckshot, and removed it. It had struck his forehead near the edge of the scalp and glided over the bone to the top of his head. I handed it to him with the knife, he then said, "thank you!" hung his cap on one side of his head, and walked off with a little saucy swagger, whistling "Yankee Doodle." Next morning we found more cannon mounted on platforms grinning down on us from over the "stockade." At this time as all others, stories of exchange were plenty in camp, so I went up to Charlie Millers, the Boston boot and shoe man, and told him that the rebs had at length agreed upon a cartel of exchange for us. He asked me if it was true? I replied that I had seen the cartel myself, but he need not take my word for it, he could see for himself, so he came down to my part of the camp with me, and I pointed to the cannon mounted during the night. "Sold" said

Charlie. "But I guess it's a fact when you came to see me down to Boston. We'll have a codfish and cranberry pie at my expense."

Chapter X

Kind reader, allow me to say a word in connection with the last described incidents, for my fellow prisoners. After these events, the rebels were desirous of visiting dire vengeance upon the leaders of this "forlorn hope." They offered large rewards and liberty to anyone who would betray the leaders.

After this time, and before the day of our release, hundreds of men who knew the secret that the rebels desired to know, died of cold and slow starvation, and of camp diseases. Hundreds and thousands lingered long enough to breathe out a few years of agony, but in the enjoyment of liberty, yet there was found not one to betray a single leader of this forlorn hope.

Bleak cold winds, and rain without any or adequate shelter, gibbering idiocy, raving insanity, starvation, despair and death, were there all of them shapes hot from hell, all of them evoked by Jeff Davis's necromancy. And they stood side by side with honor, and all--everyone preferred that to liberty and life, with dishonor! Need I say more? Only this: if I could express myself "in thoughts that speak and words that burn" with eloquence, I could do no more than justice to those men, the dead and living, but I feel and know my weakness in the presence of the subject and so right here I will stop and resume my story. The N.C. veteran regiment after this, boarded the train and left. They went, they saw, they got whipped--by the Negro raiders. What was left of them were soon returned to camp duty. A few days after their return an incident occurred, which was a horrible and unprovoked atrocity. It had been raining, and in the upper part of the camp there were several pools of water. At one of these some rods distant from the dead line, a Negro soldier was washing his handkerchief.

A portion of the veteran regiment were on duty. Two of them met on their beat, one of them said to the other, "See that black? Goddamn him! I'm going to shoot him!" I was standing near at the time, but had no idea the fiend meant it, neither did the Negro who must have heard him. The guard then deliberately cocked his gun, raised it to his face, took deliberate aim, fired and sent a ball through the Negro's heart killing him instantly. Thus he wiped out his disgrace of being whipped by a 'nigger?' How I wanted to ask if that was a sample of "Southern chivalry" but I was sure if I did that I would share the Negro's fate, so think of the old adage, "discretion being the better part of valor" I said nothing--out loud.

Sometime in the latter part of January or 1st of February '65, Mr. Merrill, whom I stated was from Michigan (I wish to amend that statement, by saying from that state or Wisconsin) was selected by the rebels, to take his assistants with him and conduct through to our lines a lot of sick and wounded prisoners. The reader will please recollect that Mr. Merrill was ward master of the hospital ward against which our adobe house was built. I will now give briefly my impressions of that gentleman. He was a man in every respect. Physically he was well built, about the medium height, a man who ladies would call handsome, and yet he would not excite the envy of his own sex, so that they would class his good looks as effeminate. He was intelligent, brave and kind hearted. An incident

I will briefly narrate illustrative of his nerve and pluck. On the day that the regulators took charge of the inside government of the camp, it was determined to first arrest the leaders of the ruffians, Howard and Turner. After quite a long debate on the best mode of making the arrest, no one seemed anxious to undertake the job, which was supposed to be extra hazardous, as both Howard and Turner were supposed to be fearless as well as desperate villains, and had the advantage of a thorough organization of men of their class to back them, and as they were defiant, there was indeed some reason to be careful. At this juncture Merrill said, "Men if you will leave this to me I will choose one man to go with me, and he and I will make the arrest." This was agreed to, he chose a man and the two arming themselves with a club for each, they went down into the part of the camp occupied by the ruffians, and walked up to what appeared to be the headquarters of the ruffians, and there sat Howard with his coat off near the door of his tent. Merrill and his friend had agreed, if necessary, to sell their lives in the undertaking, as dearly as possible, but to accomplish their task or die in the attempt. They had no show of authority as had the regulators at Andersonville by the presence of a file of rebel soldiers. Howard was expecting a demonstration and had his men standing ready--but it came upon him in an unexpected manner. His lieutenant, Turner, slunk away and hid in some hole. The two men walked without halting or hesitation up in front of Howard. Merrill pointed his weapon and asked, "Is your name Howard?" He answered that it was. "We want you" said Merrill. Howard raised to his feet, looked over his comrades, and none seemed to wish to interfere, so he asked "will you let me get my coat?" "Certainly" answered Merrill.

Howard then put on his coat and stepped between the two men and was taken to court. Shortly after Turner in disguise was dragged from his hole. The two men were tried, convicted of murder and sentenced to be hung. This would have been their fate had it not been for the treachery or carelessness of Major Gee the prison commandant. Should this narrative ever reach the eye of Mr. Merrill, and he recollect the name of his companion when Howard was arrested, he will also find where to address him. Mr. Merrill was the presiding judge in the trials in camp.

His rulings and decisions were not much hampered by law technicalities, processes, or precedents but were characterized by decorum, dignity, justice and firmness. The upper floor of his ward was reserved for a court room, and was furnished by the rebels with as much wood as the hospital ward. He and his assistants were furnished with food greatly superior both in quantity and quality to the ordinary prison fare, as were all the hospital stewards, ward master, waiters and in addition to this, his upper room being used as a court room, none but he and his assistants were allowed to enter, except when court was being held. Thus as it were, he had forced upon him a good comfortable room, plenty of hospitable bed clothes, enough of wood for a constant good fire. As soon as Mr. Merrill found he was to take charge of the sick who were to be sent home, he requested the rebel surgeon in charge, to have appointed in place of himself and assistants, to take charge of this ward, myself, Burton and Magavern. On Merrill's recommendation we were appointed and accepted charge of the hospital, with all its benefits and prerogatives. The judicial ermine of Merrill fell gracefully upon the shoulders of Burton. The change into the hospital was a happy one for me, for my lung tubes and lungs were fast relapsing into a condition of bronchial pneumonia, of which I had had so terrible an experience at Danville, VA, the previous winter. Here I was under the care of a rebel physician, had comfortable quarters and comparatively good food, all I think just in time to save my life. Yet it made me feel bad, and almost ashamed to enjoy all this comparative luxury, when hundreds of my comrades all around were gradually starving and freezing to death. I will now relate a few incidents of life in this camp. Before our removal into the hospital, there occurred at our adobe a little melodrama in which I was an actor. I never was very ambitious of distinction in pugilistic honors, but by way of an accomplishment, while at school I had taken a few lessons in the noble art of self-defense, and at one time I had almost mastered the technicalities of the profession, but always was more fitted for the position of referee, second or spectator, than principal in a prize ring. It was the habit of the members of our mess to slip out for wood with any detail that was not full, and carry wood for ourselves.

For awhile, we had been unusually successful, and had more wood than we could store away in our adobe and leave us sleeping room, so we piled it up outside and left a guard over it, and when all, except the guard lay down to sleep.

"Cock-eye" was on guard. On the preceding evening a whole company of Irishmen, who had been captured were brought in.

During the night, I was awakened by an angry talk between an Irishman and "Cock-eye." They soon came to blows. I never liked to see a fight, so I sprang up, went out and endeavored to separate the combatants, but soon received a stinging blow in the face by another Irishman who had came up with the idea that we were doubling on his countryman. I turned upon my assailant, and for a few moments I think that myself and antagonist would have made reputable, central figures for a prize ring. I felt greatly encouraged, for I seemed to be the champion of the crowd, which had by this time assembled. Everyone was calling me by name and lustily cheering me. I could not prove recreant to such an enthusiastic and unanimous constituency, so I got down to my very best work, and felt sure of conquering my adversary when someone caught me by the feet and pulled me down, and gave me a severe kick in the side. The man who pulled me down was immediately felled by a club, and the crowd walked over us. I managed to crawl to the outside of the crowd, and there learned that a whole company of Irish had attacked us, the trouble all originating in "Cock-eye's" objecting to the first Irishman carrying off our wood.

The rallying call of the regulators was given; they poured in from all directions, and the Irish company was driven off.

Never-the-less our wood pile suffered, for it furnished both sides of the combat with weapons.

Next morning I felt sore, but took my accustomed walk, which brought me alongside of the Irish company. As their roll was being called, I stopped to hear the names. At length, to my surprise, my name was called, and to my further astonishment a tall, brawny Irishman answered "here."

He had a red handkerchief around his head, and was considerably bruised. I stepped up to him and asked if that was his name? He answered as if there was nothing in the name to be ashamed of, and I think he was right--"yes sur." A mystery to me was beginning to unravel itself. Why if everybody were cheering me, why had they let some one run in behind me and pull me down during the fight? I then asked him if he was in a little bit of a row down by that adobe last night?

He answered still more emphatically "I was sur." I told him that that was my name also, and that I was in that row too, and thought as everyone was cheering me, that I had more friends than anybody."

His face brightened and extending his hand he said: "Be Jabers so thought oie, but howley mithers Moses how ye sthrike from the showther my bye; geis yer hond."

After that he and I were fast friends, but, poor fellow, he could not stand prison life.

Over a month later he was brought into our ward in a dying condition. We did everything we could for him, but his bones lie beneath the clayey sod in this prison "city of the dead."

We all knew that the fate of the Confederacy had by this time passed beyond even a forlorn hope, that its doom was sealed. It was only a question of time, yet about this time Jeff Davis made a speech to the citizens and soldiers to this city. We could hear his voice, but not his articulations. I afterward read his speech in a paper published at Salisbury, and in the speech he claimed that the confederacy was in a better condition for defense, and was near victory and independence.

"Another sharp and decisive victory and all will be won."

I do not believe there was one other man in the Confederacy at that time so ignorant of the situation as to believe one word of what he said.

Now from this we must conclude that he was either impressed with that insane hallucination at the time, or deliberately lied.

Another incident that I recall is this:

In February came a sudden thaw, with a heavy, warm, continuous rain, hundreds and thousands of prisoners had been wholly without shelter. So many of them dug holes in the ground from four to six feet deep, then at right angles from the vertical hole they dug out a lane. This then was their only shelter from the winter winds. During this thaw and rain, many of these holes had caved in. I enquired diligently to find if their occupants had escaped, but I could not find any that knew, neither did I know of any hole being investigated to find if it contained the corpse of its occupant. The reason for this appeared to be a languid and stupid apathy, induced by sickness, suffering, starvation and despair. They appeared to care but little for their own fate, or for the fate of anybody. I think that since that night, many of these habitations of men have been graves, in which lie many of our unknown dead.

During the severest cold of the winter many were without shelter and a result these starved men were frequently found in the mornings, frozen to death. They with others, who had died during the nights, were picked up and carried into the morgue in "dead hours."

In the morning an army team and wagon would be backed up to the door of the morgue, by some Negroes. Then the Negroes would "cord" in the dead as long as the wagon box would hold them, then drive them to the burying ground.

One morning while they, as usual, were loading up the wagon with the dead, they were swinging a body preparitively to throwing it up on the load of dead, when it began to kick. The Negroes dropped the man in horror, starting back with protruding eyes and straightening wool, looking like the picture of ludicrous consternation. According to a certain colored preacher's theology--so runs the story:

The origin of the white race was from Cain. Adam and Eve were both black, so was Cain and Abel. One day Cain he kill Abel, den de good Lowd he said to Cain, "Wha is di brudder Abel?" Cain say he dunno, De Lowd he say again, "wha is di brudder?" Cain he get scared and tund white."

A person seeing these Darkies at this time, would yield the point and admit it a phenomenon on which the Negro preacher evidently founded his theory of the origin of the white race. The poor soldier had been chilled to the point of death and had been brought in a supposed corpse, but the vital spark of heavenly flame had not quite fled and the warmth of the "dead house" had partially revived him. He was carried in a hospital and restoratives exhibited and applied. I believe he fully recovered.

During the early and middle part of February a great many of the sick were taken from prison, and we were told that their destination was home. This argued well for an early exchange for all of us, but we had learned from sad experience the danger of entertaining a delusive hope. So we were finishing a long and large tunnel, to which our ward of the hospital was furnishing every bit of candle or fat we could save, to make light in the tunnel for the workers. It was the agreement that on the night of the first of March the tunnel should be opened. Everything was arranged as to who should take precedence in passing out. It was so arranged that the tunnel was to open in a railroad cut. Outside the railroad guard lines and picket. It was hoped that this tunnel would almost wholly empty the prison. This tunnel, however, was never used, was never opened on the outside. The long wished for, and long hoped for day of our liberty was beginning to dawn, and so the tunnel was never needed.

Chapter XI

On the 22nd day of February, 1865, the anniversary of Washington's Birthday--I think it was never so joyfully celebrated--came the glorious news. A gentle breeze was blowing up from the orange groves of the Isles and beautiful shores of the sunny south, a genial warmth that told in that clime the near approach of spring.

A Confederate officer rode into camp, and after commanding the attention of the prisoners, called out something like the following language, as he rode through the camp. "Fall into ranks men, all of you who are able for a short march. You will be marched to Greensboro, where you will take the cars by way of Raleigh to Goldsboro, at which place you will be paroled and sent within your lines at Wilmington. Special provision has been made for your sick, and you would be furnished with transportation from here, but all the spare cars in the Confederacy are being used elsewhere to transport your men to points of exchange or parole." Oh, what a shout there went up from that camp! Men on whose brows were already gathering the dews of death, staggered to their feet and into ranks, and shouted "home" "freedom." All seemed intoxicated, insane with joy. Many expressed their joy in sobs and tears. All who were able to move fell into ranks, and the command, "right face, forward march" was given. Then we marched "out from the jaws of death" out from hell, all that was left of us. Many staggered out, only to fall by the wayside and die.

"Glad to breathe one free breath, Though on the lips of death."

Oh dear! My recollections of these times is again carrying me beyond my depth, so I will change the subject for a little while. I presume that I have always been more or less troubled by the disease, agnosticism. In fact, I am sort of a doubting Thomas. In looking back over my life I think I can find plenty of reasons for this. For example when a small boy, I heard a fellow named Charley Hornbook tell an uncle of mine, W.J. Caldwell, that he, Hornbook, had more money than he wanted, so near a certain grove he had thrown away a whole sack full of his money. In the expressive language of the period, I "took it all in." I will never tell how often afterward I played truant to hunt for that money, but I can say, that there was not a foot of ground within several hundred feet of that grove that I did not fully explore, and when I did finally give up the hunt, it was with a great loss of faith in the character for veracity of mankind in general, and Charley Hornbook in particular. I had some such experience in Dixie. The previous spring, at Danville, VA, the rebels wished to remove us to Andersonville, GA, so they told us we were to be taken to City Point for exchange, so they paroled us requiring a parole of honor, not to attempt an escape until we reached City Point. They marched us with scarcely any guard to Petersburg. Here we were placed on a train of cars, heavy guards over us. It looked suspicious and made us feel a little blue, but when an engine backed down to the wrong end of the train to take us to City Point, we knew our destination. Our despair was fixed, and the rebs jubilant over their "Yankee trick." We were struck dumb with horror at our situation, for we had heard of Andersonville. I rallied a moment and said to Alex Forbes, a comrade of Co. I "that I could feel the joke, but could not see Point."

Then again at Andersonville when we were being sent to Charleston we were again assured that we were being taken to points of exchange, and afterward had been landed in, if possible, a worse place than Andersonville i.e. Florence, SC.

Now when we were marched out of Salisbury, I was not sure by any means that the rebels meant to parole us, but might be taking us to a place of security from the Union armies, so I took the earliest opportunity of making my escape. This was easily accomplished, for we were not closely guarded. In fact we were now talked to and treated more like men, for we were under the charge of some of their soldiers from the front. A short time after I had escaped, I was confronted by three men, who told me that they were Union men and I staid that night with them. They told me this was an honest move on the rebels and meant parole or exchange. It had been raining all day, but was still warm.

On next morning I took their advice and that evening I rejoined the prisoners at Greensboro--the only time I ever voluntarily surrendered until I married, since which time I am used to it.

On the following day we were put aboard the cars, and sent to Goldsboro.[36] Here we were bivouacked in a forest near the village. On the following morning a rebel officer approached me with the inquiry if I "could write?" From the nature and manner of his question, I inferred that in that latitude it was an accomplishment of which I might justly be proud of, so I answered "yes, with a little practice I may be able to rival the chirography of the great Horace Greely."[37] He handed me pen, ink and paper. Supposing that I had struck a southern autograph fiend who was taking this method to collect the names of great men, I fired a Latin sentence that I had committed to memory at school, at him and subscribed my name, and handed it to him. When he had examined it, he said it would do, and he wanted me. Five other men were similarly selected, and we were marched off two and two and placed in three offices, and were required to take a parole of honor not to attempt to escape, and then were given the privilege of the camp, on condition that we parole our fellow prisoners. After counseling together we could see no harm in doing it, so we consented to do the work. Immediately there was detailed two rebel soldiers, a cook and a waiter. Of course this menial service would have been done by the slaves, had they dared trust them with us. We were now furnished with blank parole rolls, one to be made out for the original, the other for a duplicate. The prisoners were then marched up to these officers in three columns, and the Company, Regiment and State of each one was asked and recorded, then their names, and as the last stroke of the pen was being made in writing their names, they were required to touch the pen.

This was their signature to the parole. To us, thus employed, corn meal, sweet potatoes and bacon was furnished in abundance. I had my cook prepare my cornmeal and bake it into "pones" as it was received, for I was not yet sure but there would be "a slip 'twixt the cup and the lip." So a few days after, when we were through, or nearly through paroling the prisoners, I had a bushel sack full of these "pones." One day when we were nearly through paroling the prisoners, and were hoping that no more would be brought into camp until we could leave, a distant picket firing was heard. Great commotion and evident anxiety was apparent among the rebels, and we were hurriedly huddled onto a train of cars.

Those who had been paroled on the previous days, had been sent off as fast as paroled, so that now there were comparatively but few of us.

While paroling the prisoners we were constantly in contact with rebel officers and men, who had met with us face to face on the battle field. Many of them had been prisoners in the north and whose faces blushed with shame, when they beheld our condition. These men treated us kindly, this class with a few exceptions, always did.

But somewhere in the "Confederacy" there was a fiend, and it evidently had to a great extent supreme power and to almost its fullest extent its malignancy was expended upon the helpless prisoners. When a man was appointed over the prisoners, it seemed to be always with an especial reference to his fiendish, heartless, villainous character. If there are those who doubt this, I invite them but to look at the character of the men in the south who had charge of the prisons.

First that miserable Scion of sycophancy, cruelty and bigotry, the Rev. Gen. Winder,[38] Turner of Libby; Jim Chris of Danville, Wirz, of Andersonville and Gee, of Salisbury. That such men were there by Jeff Davis' personal schemes and machinations, I have seen the best of proof.

So Jefferson Davis is that fiend. I feel that I do myself honor to revere the name of such a man as Alexander Stephens.[39]--Peace to his ashes, and I would have felt proud to have taken him by the hand, for I knew that he was ever an honorable and chivalrous foe or friend, or even Robert Tombs or Wade Hampton or many other men who were and are bitter rebels, but who, notwithstanding have many noble traits of character, but preserve me ever from a sight of such a foul and unhuman fiend as Jefferson Davis.

As a rule, the people of the south were and are generous, chivalrous, hospitable and brave. Some of these qualities are remarkably exemplified in the South while they are neither more chivalrous nor brave, than those of the North. We, of the North I think, must yield the palm of victory to the South in generous hospitality. These qualities belong to their poor as well as their rich, to their uneducated as well as to their educated, but all such rules admit exceptions. They were cursed by the blight of slavery, and all its demoralizing influences.

An English author says of Napoleon Bonaparte that "in the name of Brutus he grasped without remorse, and wore without shame the diadem of the Caesars."

The Rebellion demonstrates that even the best of men, under the touch of personal interest and the influence of a false education may commit a great wrong and not be aware of it. So the Southern people under the holy name of "Democracy" inaugurated a slave holders Rebellion of "Chivalry" they held in slavery a weaker race, and bad as was their cause in which they fought so bravely, their leader was unworthy of even such a cause, and leader and cause unworthy of such brave and chivalrous men.

> "But here my Muse her wing maun cour
> Sic flights as far beyond her power." [40]

Let's see--O yes!

I had just got aboard the train, with my bushel sack full of corn "pones" and my haversack full of sweet potatoes and bacon. Soon the steam engine whistled and we were off. After a ride of several hours the train stopped and we were ordered off and to fall into ranks.

I looked down the track and saw a white flag waving, and under it a Federal and Confederate officer, standing one on either side of the track. We were marched down the track, and between the two aforesaid officers, and as we passed we were counted by them. When I passed between the two officers I was still staggering along under the load of my sack of "pones." These "pones" were something of the size, shape, consistence and weight, of a 12 pound cannon shot, only the pones were a little flattened on one side.

I now began to experience a strange thrill of hope. I looked further down the track and saw a beautiful specimen of the decorative art, in the shape of an arch, woven of evergreens. It was a beautiful structure, and reflected great cred on the hearts and hands of the colored soldiers, whose heartfelt pity for our condition prompted it, whose heads designed it, and whose hands erected it, as a triumphal arch for us, who had thus at last triumphed over our misery, to pass under. On either side of this triumphal arch was a line of guards extending into the forest on either side as far as we could see.

These lines were composed entirely of colored soldiers. This was our picket line. It seemed to me just then as if I was passing from the confines of a Homers Odesic Hades into beautiful Elysian fields,[41] full of eternal glories and happiness.

There was an almost complete fruition of the brightest hopes, of the wildest fancy that ever soared with unclipped wing from a Southern prison.

To us gentle breezes were wafted up from the south, ladened with the odor of orange blossoms and heliotrope which stirred the branches of the trees. I looked up, almost expecting to find what it was the rustle of "an angel's wing." The Negro guards seemed to us to be bright Angels, meeting us on the brink of the "beautiful Shore" to welcome us to home and happiness.

Still I staggered along under the weight of my sack of corn "pone" until I had passed under the evergreen arch, and within the Federal lines.

Just then a military band struck up "Hail Columbia." It had been long since I heard that grand old patriotic tune, so I stepped out of ranks and sat down by my sack of "pones" to rest, listen to the music, and still the beating of my heart, which seemed to evince a disposition to jump out of my mouth.

This was about the 8th of March, '65. I had been captured at Chickamauga battle, Sept. 20th, '63,

Think of the fable of Prometheus[42] as he lay chained to the cold rocks of the Caucasian mountains, the links of Vulcan's chain festering his flesh, the vultures tearing his flesh, continually enduring the agony of death, but because he was a god he could not die.

Well, this had been about my fix for nearly one and one half years--except that I was not a god, and don't think Prometheus was either, but now it is all over. Here my soliloquy took something like this from "Here you are old boy. Saved at last in spite of fears and agnosticism."

Then the music of the band ceased and then I could hear all around me the music of the early song birds of the Sunny South.

The trees were budding into new life, and the early flowers were beginning to blossom. Before me was a beautiful green sward of blue grass. Here a colored soldier who had not yet forgotten his plantation manners differentially approached me.

"Mossa I begs yer padon, but hab you some con bread to spa?"

I said "yes sir, my friend and brother" and handed him a piece, and another colored soldier came up with a similar request and was made happy, just then several of them started on a run for me, when I took out all the pones one by one and sent them rolling over the green grass like bolls in a ten pin alley. Other prisoners were doing the same with their corn bread--if they had any, and such a scramble for corn bread I never expect to see again. The poor fellows were evidently tired of camp fare and were longing for the "flesh pots" and "compones" of their old cabin homes.

From here we were marched by easy stages--those who were able to march, until we arrived at a beautiful grove of live oaks in the suburbs of Wilmington. There were erected tables on which was spread food for us. As the tables all seemed full or crowded, I sat down to rest and wait, leaning myself against the trunk of a tree. I had not waited long when an officer, a Captain approached me and asked if I wanted something to eat?

I told him "yes, but could wait until the tables were not so crowded." He left, but soon returned with a large dish covered by Army crackers, boiled meats, oranges and a tin cup full of hot, rich coffee.

I was about to say that I thought this was a feast, fit for a God or Angels, but recollecting that manna is the food of Angels, and that mankind being more material than Angels, requires more substantial food, hence, probably the longing for the flesh pots of Egypt.[43]

I enjoyed this feast, and thought it fit for any man. Perhaps when we all get to be Angels, we can appreciate a feast of manna, and may not be so much like those old Jewish fellows in the wilderness. I don't think that I would have blamed them much.

This Captain seemed pleased because I enjoyed the food, and asked me how I felt?

I told him I felt just as though I had died and gone to Heaven, and that an Archangel was ministering unto me. If that Captain is still alive I would be glad if he knew that I never forgot his kindness.

Chapter XI End notes

36   *Greensboro-Raleigh-Goldsboro-Wilmington*. McHenry mentions these North Carolina cities while marking the prisoners' 225-mile journey from the Salisbury camp to Wilmington, a port city on the Atlantic Ocean where they were released on March 8, 1865.

37   *Horace Greeley* (1811-1872) was a famous American author and reformer who founded and edited the influential *New York Tribune*.

38   Rev. General *John H. Winder* (1800-1865) was a Confederate general noted for commanding prisoner-of-war camps throughout the South during the Civil War. Lieutenant *Thomas Pratt Turner* was the first commandant of the Libby prisoner-of-war camp.

39   *Alexander Stephens* (1812-1883) served as the only vice-president of the Confederate States from 1861 to 1865. *Robert Augustus Toombs* (1810-1885) was an organizer of the Confederacy and its first secretary of state. *Wade Hampton III* (1818-1902) was a South Carolina politician and Confederate general during the Civil War.

Alexander Stephens, Confederate Vice-President

40 *"But her my Muse her wing maun cour..."* McHenry is quoting from Robert Burns' poem, *Tam O' Shanter: A Tale*.

41 The *Elysian Fields* is a mythological land of perfect happiness where the souls of the heroic and virtuous Greeks rest in peace.

42 In Greek mythology, Zeus, the king of the gods, punished the Titan *Prometheus* by binding him to a rock by chains forged by *Vulcan*, god of blacksmithing. Prometheus' crime was stealing fire and giving it to humanity. Every day Zeus sent an eagle to feed on

Prometheus' liver, which grew back overnight only to be devoured again the next day.

43   The *flesh pots of Egypt* were vessels for cooking meat used by the ancient Egyptians. In the biblical story of the Exodus from Egypt, the freed Israelites grew weary of the hunger and uncertainty of wandering in the desert and hankered after the former security of their Egyptian enslavement when they ate regularly from the flesh pots.

Chapter XII

The night following we found comfortable quarters in deserted stores and warehouses along the wharf on the bank of Cape Fear River[44] in Wilmington.

Next morning rations were issued to us. Some of the poor fellows did not seem to realize that they were yet free and in a land of plenty, and friends, but an insane fear of starvation seemed to overpower their reason. So they would resort to tricks to procure more food than was necessary or they could use, then eat what they wanted and guard the rest, as a miser would his gold. They ate more than their digestive organs could assimilate, and in their weakened condition, indigestion, disease and death speedily followed.

When I reached the wharf Magovern, Burton and all my chums had gone. I searched a long time among the prisoners before I could find anyone that I knew.

Here we had to remain for several days waiting for transportation to Annapolis, MD.

One morning while wandering aimlessly about, I met a comrade of my regiment, Geo. H. Love. I was overjoyed to meet my old comrade and friend, but oh, what he had suffered since we had parted at Charleston, SC. He seemed in every way a wreck of his former self. With him were two men with whom he became acquainted at Florence, SC, Frank Seguin and a Mr. Shurtz, both good men. I believe they were from Kankakee, Illinois. Frank Seguin was one of the jolliest, good fellows that I had ever the good fortune to meet. We four formed ourselves together into a mess and came through together to St. Louis. A few days later we succeeded in crowding ourselves on a river transport, and sailed down the river to the bar at the mouth of the river. The tide was out and we could not cross the bar. Outside the bar lay two ocean steamers. Our boat not being able to get across the bar, we had to await the incoming of the tide, so we were landed on the north shore, and for a while amused ourselves by wading out on the bar and gathering small oysters, shells, etc.

At length the tide began to come in, and we were soon aboard our boat, across the bar and upon the heavy billows of Old Ocean.

We were soon transferred to the ocean steamer. By next morning all were aboard, then the anchor was shipped and soon we were on our way up the coast. The other steamer followed about five miles in our wake.

We were crowded into a large room or apartment of the steamer that had evidently been used to transport a lot of horses, and although it had been washed, it was damp, and an unpleasant, ammoniacal odor, and a want of ventilation made it rather sickening.

When we reached Cape Hatteras,[45] we encountered quite a gale, many became sea sick, and this was too much for some of our poor fellows, for two or three of them died during the passage.

At best the experience for the first time of being "rocked into the cradle of the deep" is not as pleasant as the same operation in the cradle of infancy, nor is the howling wind at all comparable to a mother's lullaby.

I was beginning to be somewhat unsteady in the gastric regions myself, and somewhat desperate, when a soldier with more experience than good sense proposed to me that we reach out from an open side hatch or window "catch on" to the rigging of the ship and climb up on the hurricane deck. I asked him if it could be safely done?

"Certainly" said he.

He easily swang himself into the rigging and climbed up like a squirrel. I also swang myself into the rigging and climbed up, not so much like a squirrel as a lubber.

The ship was rocking fearfully, and by the time I reached the railing of the deck my head was spinning like a top and I was blind. In another moment I would have been food for sharks but the fellow seeing my condition shouted to a sailor nearby.

"Here shipmate."

The sailor came running up, and he and my friend caught me by the arms and lifted me over the railing onto the deck.

My companion seemed surprised that I should attempt to climb up the rigging, and said: "What did you do that for?"

I told him that he had proposed it, said it was practicable, and that I wanted out of that hole.

He said he didn't suppose anyone but a sailor would attempt such a thing under the circumstances, and also told me that he was an old "skipper," a nautical term for sea captain.

Well a danger that is over is not long dreaded especially if it is unforeseen.

From this place we could see in all directions and could see the other steamer following. The wind blew a perfect gale, and there appeared to be a line of rocky and narrow islands between us and the shore over which the waves brake in great fury. I had heard that Cape Hatteras was the most dangerous part of our Atlantic coast and that March was the most dangerous month of the year, and might have been somewhat uneasy had I been able to discover any anxiety on the part of the crew of the steamer, and my companion whom I had just learned was an old sailor.

My companion, the ex "skipper" now informed me that he had met his regiment at Wilmington, and as good luck would have it, it was pay day and he had drawn his pay and had money, so I accepted his invitation and went down to dinner with him.

When again we came on deck we noticed some anxiety and excitement among the officers and crew. I could not see but we were as near all right as at any time since we had encountered the gale.

We were soon informed that the other steamer was going to pieces on the rocks, and that it would be certain death to our crew and passengers to even attempt a rescue.

The ship went to pieces on the breakers and nearly every man on board perished. At that time this incidental sent a thrill of horror all through the north.[46]

This was a sad ending for the poor fellows. Many hundreds were in the steamer, many of whom had underwent the horrors of a long and cruel imprisonment, buoyed up alone by the hope of meeting the loved ones at home. The fruition of their tree of hope ripens, they reach forth to grasp it. Father, mother, sister, brother, wife, child or sweetheart were never again to be pressed to their loving hearts. They sank beneath the wave and hundreds of hearts and homes were made desolate. But was it not better for them to die thus by the inevitable hand of fate than to sink under the cruelty of our fellow men?

On next morning we passed Fortress Monroe,[47] sailed up Chesapeake Bay and landed at Annapolis, MD.

Here we marched, a few at a time along a gang way into a building, said to be one of the Naval Academy buildings. Here in the first room we entered we were ordered to strip ourselves of our clothing (usually filthy, pediculous rags) which were pitched out at a side door, into a fire and burned up.

When I found out the fate of the old clothes, I said:

"Hold on!"

The fellow stopped and I went into the pants pocket, took out a few Confederate bills and fifteen cents of US scrip, then told him to go ahead with his bonfire.

We then enjoyed the luxury of a thorough, disinfecting bath, after which we passed under the hands of a barber, who clipped our hair, shampooed, and shaved us.

Oh how our finger nails grew after that! After we left the barbers we were taken into a room, and furnished with a complete suit of new clothes, including a new hat, and shoes.

After this we were marched into another room, and sat down to a good dinner. Now we knew better than any others how to appreciate these good things, for we had so long felt the need of them. Frank said: "Boys, we have been born with a silver spoon in our mouth, after all."

Shurtz answered: "At last we've shaken the fetters from our heels."

"Bless my riggin!" said George, "if that ain't so."

It was my time, so I rose to the occasion to remark that we four, and many more, being to the manor born, could stand lots of this kind of treatment from Uncle Sam, bless his old heart, and confusion to Jeff Davis.

This was eighteen years ago, and the experience of this time has not fully realized the hopes of our country's patriotic men, but it has taught us a lesson. A lesson of the grandeur of peace, and the evil of war. Peace brings us statesmanship unselfish, noble and grand. War is the opportunity of unscrupulous, selfish, shrewdness and unholy ambition. Peace develops a Lincoln; war a Grant, one will preserve the liberties of our institutions, the other would subserve them to its own personal ends. The motto of peace is equal and "Exact, right and justice to all." The motto of a large class that our late war left in power is "any means to maintain ourselves in power."

For the support of a wealthy corporate power or monopoly,[48] they have already granted powerful franchises that are incompatible in their nature, with free institutions. For example, a perpetuity of corporate life, rendering nugatory our laws against primo geniture, another an assumption of corporate power, to wrest from the people of the country their control through congress of inter-state and inter-national commerce, thus leaving its control all for the benefit of these corporations. So much is this now the case, that two men unscrupulous as they are, and controlling these and other franchises, can now raise more of a revenue from off the industries of this country than can be done by any other two kings, prince or potentates in any other country on the globe today. There are franchises lost to the people by their blind trust in a scum from off the seething, boiling, scalding cauldron of war. The franchises of the people are held in trust by their rulers and representatives and when one of these proves recreant to the trust, and gives away the franchises of the people, he often looks wise and says, "We need a centralized government, property is not safe enough."

Oh, how like the whine of an overseer when his whip does not cut deep enough into the quivering flesh.

Oh, how hard it is to choke bull dog men from the bone of office which they only hold to abuse.

Turn back, oh, tide of time, and again strike from the wrists of slaves 4,000,000 shackles, but do not again fasten 40,000,000 on the arms of our industries.

Shortly after our dinner, we were marched by an office where an officer asked us our names, company, regiment, state, date of capture etc., then we were required to sign a roll, and we were handed a sum of money which we were told was commutation for rations, after which we were marched a short distance into camp.

My comrade George H. Love had had a brother who fell, I think in one of the battles of Bull Run. Here he heard that his other and only brother had also fallen in battle. His mother, a widow, and a perfect Angel of a little sister, thinking him dead also had sunk and died under the blow. Poor George, his cup of bitterness was full. He yet lives, at Dix, Jefferson Co., Illinois.

A few days later the Illinois, Iowa, and Missouri soldiers were ordered to St. Louis, MO. We were put on board a train and started on the B. & O. Railroad[49] for the west. After we got started Frank Segum and myself, feeling like birds out of a cage turned ourselves loose for a little fun on the road.

On the south side of the Potomac River, opposite a little town, a freight train had been wrecked on the main track just before our arrival. Our train could not pass until the debris had been cleared away, so Frank and I tried to get over to the town, but we found guards on the ferry boat who would not allow us to pass. We also learned that the fishermen and boatmen had orders not to take any of us across, so we bought a boat of a Negro for five dollars and rowed ourselves across and put up at a hotel. After dinner we "took in" the town. When we had seen all the sights we recrossed the river, sold our boat to the same darky of whom we had bought it, for four dollars.

We just arrived at the train in time not to be left. Next we got off at a perfect little nest of a city, in the panhandle of Maryland, in a mountainous district called Cumberland.[50] It is a beautiful place, situated in a lovely little valley and surrounded by mountains. I think that if I had lived in such a beautiful and romantic a locality as Cumberland I would have broken out all over into poetry worse than a case of confluent smallpox.

Frank and I again reached the train after taking a view of the city.

We at length arrived at Bellaire, Ohio, the bridge being down, we were ferried across. While waiting for the ferry, Frank and I "did" the nail and other iron works on the Virginia side. Here I witnessed rather a thrilling incident. There was being guarded, a man in rebel uniform. What his crime was I could not learn, but suddenly he broke from the guards and ran toward an adjacent mountain, and began its steep ascent. The soldiers began firing at him, and the fugitive and soldiers passed out of sight, but there could be heard for some time, the occasional report of a musket. I never learned the result of the chase, but I could not control my sympathy, and unless he was a murderer or a thief, I hoped he would make his escape.

When we had arrived over into Bellaire, the train that was to bear us westward was not on hand, so all the boys began to look around. They soon discovered a bonanza, and it was not long before they were nearly all bonanza kings. The bonanza was a whole train of cars from Cincinnati sitting on a side track, and loaded with whisky. Several barrels of it was soon rolled out of the cars, up-ended, the heads knocked out, and the boys helped themselves with their tin cups and canteens. Hence the aforesaid bonanza kings of kings.

Here Frank and I took a bath and visited a barber shop, and bought us a suit of citizens clothes. We found here an elderly gentleman who had been crippled by wounds in the service. He invited us to dinner. We went with him and were introduced to two young ladies, his daughters. They were pretty, intelligent and good musicians.

After dinner we were pleasantly entertained by the girls, by songs and piano accompaniment. Soon after, we accepted the invitation of the girls and their father to return to supper, then left and took a stroll around town.

At length we returned, and bid our fair entertainers adieu, and with their father, who had been a Major in the service, started for the depot.

When we arrived at the depot, we found to our dismay that we had at last succeeded in being left, for our train had come and gone.

The Major said to us "that's all right boys," and took us into the provost marshal's office and explained how the accident had happened, taking, in spite of us, the blame upon himself, and we were given first-class passenger tickets to St. Louis.

When we reached Columbus, Ohio, we learned that during the night we had passed our train, and we were then determined to await its coming. It was Sunday, so we concluded to go to church. I had but little choice, so I allowed Frank to select the church, and he selected the Cathedral, so we went there. When we got inside, to my surprise Frank sprinkled himself with the "howley wather" and went through the genuflections like an old timer. I looked at him with surprise and was about to remonstrate with the boy for his ill timed levity, when I caught by the look of his eye, a fact that I had not hitherto learned--Frank was a devout Catholic.

After service we went down to the depot just in time to see our train come in.

After our transfiguration by the hands of the barber and clothing, from soldiers to citizens, our chums did not for a while know us. Here we again put on our soldier clothes and did not again separate ourselves from our chums until our final parting, at St. Louis. Since that time I have of these men met only George H. Love, and him but once.

In passing through Ohio, we were everywhere reminded that we were among friends. When the citizens of any town, city or village knew that we were coming, they were always on hand with oranges, fruits of other kinds, and food. But it was at Richmond, Indiana that we were treated best. As soon as the train stopped, the city bells were rang, and the citizens turned out and almost overwhelmed us with good things to eat.

These demonstrations were almost a perfect ovation. I do not think that one of those ex-prisoners will ever forget the generous hospitality of the glorious little City of Richmond, Indiana.[51]

What remains is easily told. Through the rest of Indiana and Illinois our reception was about the same as through Ohio.

In due time we arrived at St. Louis. Here we were beset by apparently the same boot blacks, news boys, apple women, and orange girls, and Jew clothiers, theatrical bill and patent medicine advertisements that we had left behind us four years ago.

Ah! It looked like home. Here we were taken to Benton Barracks, and those of us whose term of service had expired were given furloughs, paid two month's wages, and were ordered to report to our respective State Capitals for discharge. Those whose term of service had not expired were given the same pay, a furlough and orders to report to their regiments.

Here I met Capt. Robert Harmer, of the 80th Illinois Infantry who had just arrived here from imprisonment in Dixie, and we went home together, about 50 miles southeast of St. Louis.

I will not attempt to portray the joys of meeting friends at home, it is sacred in my memory, and I draw over it the curtain of silence.

James McHenry

Late private of Co. H

22nd Illinois Infantry Volunteers

Minneapolis, Ottawa County, Kansas

James McHenry's Trip Home From Prison

Trip Home

1. Salisbury, NC
2. Greensboro, NC
3. Goldsboro, NC
4. Wilmington, NC
5. Cape Hatteras, NC
6. Fortress Monroe, VA
7. Annapolis, MD
8. Cumberland, MD
9. Bellaire, OH
10. Columbus, OH
11. Richmond, IN
12. St. Louis, MO
13. Sparta, IL

Chapter XII End notes

44 *Cape Fear River* is a 202-mile-long river that flows through the wetlands of east central North Carolina before emptying into the Atlantic Ocean at Cape Fear.

45 *Cape Hatteras* is a thin line of islands in North Carolina that arch out into the Atlantic Ocean. Known as the "Graveyard of the Atlantic," this area suffered a disproportionately high number of shipwrecks over time.

46 On March 31, 1865, the U.S. Army transport steamship, *the USS General Lyon*, sunk in rough waters off of Cape Hatteras. Approximately 500 passengers—discharged Union soldiers, paroled prisoners of war, and refugees—lost their lives. There were 29 survivors.

47 *Fort Monroe* is a seven-sided stone fort located on the Virginia shore of Chesapeake Bay. The fort guarded naval entry into the Chesapeake Bay, thereby controlling access by water to Washington D.C.

48 McHenry's verbal assault on *"wealthy corporate powers or monopoly"* is an expression of his political beliefs that the

concentration of wealth and power in post-Civil War America corrupted democracy and denied the mass of ordinary citizens the opportunity to realize the American Dream.

49 Chartered in 1827, The *B & O* (Baltimore and Ohio) Railroad is one of the oldest railroads in the United States.

50 The mountains near *Cumberland* in western Maryland are renowned for their scenic beauty.

51 *Richmond, Indiana* is located near the Ohio border 73 miles east of Indianapolis. Its population in 1860 was 6,608.

Appendix A

<u>Major Actions of the 22nd Illinois Infantry (July 1861-September 20, 1863)</u>

July 11, 1861   Stationed at Bird's Point, MO (South of Cairo, IL)

August 19, 1861   Battle of Charleston, MO

November 7, 1861   Battle of Belmont, MO

January 14, 1862   Reconnaissance mission near Columbus, KY

March 2-13, 1862   Battle of New Madrid, MO

April 8, 1862   Capture of Tiptonville, TN

May 3-9, 1862   Battle of Farmington, MS

September 9-11, 1862   Arrived in Nashville, TN

December 31, 1862-January 2, 1863   Battle of Stones River, TN

June 24-26, 1863 Battle of Liberty Gap, TN

June 24-July 3, 1863   Tullahoma Campaign, Tennessee

September 18-20, 1863   Battle of Chickamauga, GA

September 20, 1863   James McHenry captured by Confederate forces

Civil War Battles Of The 22nd Illinois Volunteer Infantry In Which James McHenry Participated

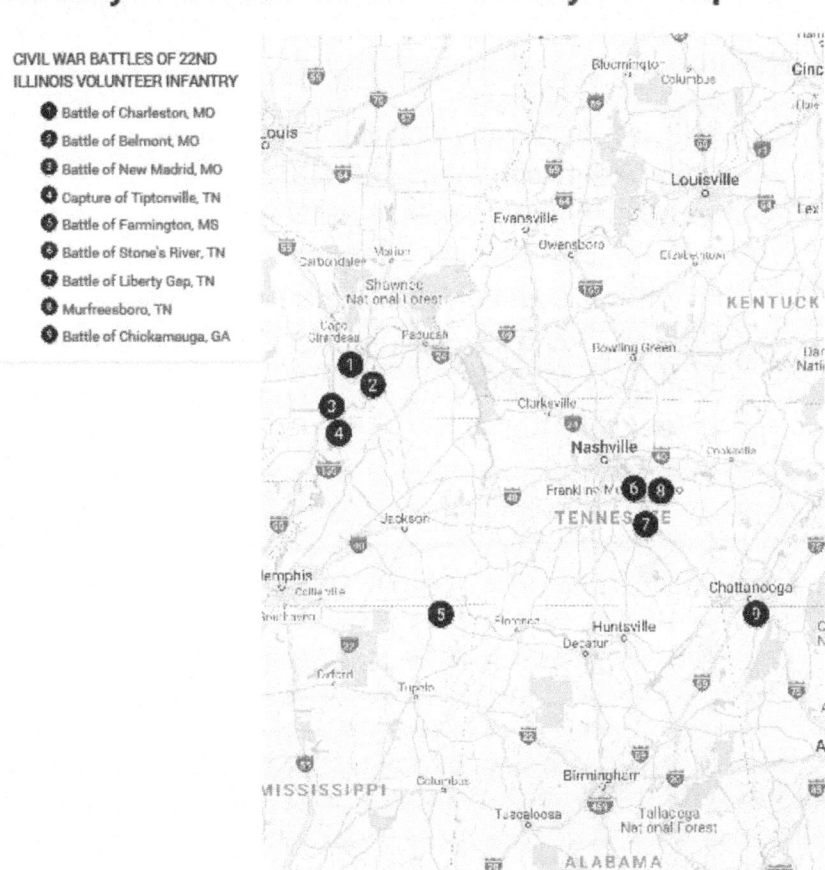

CIVIL WAR BATTLES OF 22ND ILLINOIS VOLUNTEER INFANTRY

1. Battle of Charleston, MO
2. Battle of Belmont, MO
3. Battle of New Madrid, MO
4. Capture of Tiptonville, TN
5. Battle of Farmington, MS
6. Battle of Stone's River, TN
7. Battle of Liberty Gap, TN
8. Murfreesboro, TN
9. Battle of Chickamauga, GA

Appendix B

Confederate Prisons Where James McHenry Was Incarcerated

1. **Belle Isle** (Richmond, Virginia), autumn 1863
2. **Libby** (Richmond), winter 1863-1864
3. **Danville, Virginia**, winter 1863-1864
4. **Andersonville, Georgia**, arrived March 1864
5. **Charleston, South Carolina**, late summer 1864
6. **Florence, South Carolina**, arrived September 19, escaped September 20, 1864
7. **Salisbury, North Carolina** October 1864 through February 22, 1865

CONFEDERATE PRISONER OF WAR CAMPS IN WHICH JAMES McHENRY WAS HELD

POW CAMPS
- Belle Isle, VA
- Libby, VA
- Danville, VA
- Andersonville, GA
- Charleston, SC
- Florence, SC
- Salisbury, NC

Two of Dr. McHenry's ledger books survive. The first one is dated April 17, 1871. The second is dated December 30, 1873. Both are in the Ottawa County Historical Museum in Minneapolis, KS.

Dr. McHenry's ledger page for the James Morgan family is typical of the accounts contained in both ledger books.

SELECTED BIBLIOGRAPHY

Bader, Robert Smith. *Prohibition in Kansas: A History*. Lawrence: University Press of Kansas, 1986.

Bonner, Thomas Neville. *The Kansas Doctor: A Century of Pioneering*. Lawrence: University Press of Kansas, 1959.

Brown, Louis A. *The Salisbury Prison: A Case Study of Confederate Military Prisons, 1861-1865*. Wendell, North Carolina: Avera Press, 1980.

Chalfant, William Y. *Hancock's War: Conflict on the Southern Plains*. Norman: University of Oklahoma Press, 2010.

Hertzler, Arthur E., M.D. *The Horse and Buggy Doctor*. Lincoln: University of Nebraska Press, 1938.

History of Ottawa County, Kansas, 1864-1984. 1984. Reprint, 2001.

Long, Lessel. *Twelve Months in Andersonville*. 1886. Reprint, Big Byte Books, 2015.

McHenry and Dunn's Ledger Books. April 1871 and December 1873. Ottawa County Historical Museum collection.

McMurry, Linda O. *George Washington Carver: Scientist and Symbol*. Oxford: Oxford University Press, 1981.

McNall, Scott G. *Class Formation and Kansas Populism, 1865-1900*. Chicago: University of Chicago Press, 1988.

McPherson, James. *Battle Cry of Freedom: The Civil War Era*. Oxford: Oxford University Press, 1988.

Malin, James C. *A Concern About Humanity: Notes on Reform, 1872-1912 at the National and Kansas Levels of Thought*. Lawrence: James C. Malin, 1964.

Richardson, Albert D. *The Secret Service: The Field, the Dungeon, and the Escape*. 1865. Reprint, Big Byte Books, 2015.

Sanders, Charles W. Jr. *While in the Hands of the Enemy: Military Prisons of the Civil War*. Baton Rouge: Louisiana State University Press, 2005.